Books by Beverly Plummer

FRAGRANCE
How to Make Natural Soaps, Scents and Sundries   1975

EARTH PRESENTS   1974

GIVE EVERY DAY A CHANCE   1970

FRAGRANCE

How to Make Natural Soaps, Scents and Sundries

A harvest of gift soaps made at home by Beverly Plummer

Beverly Plummer

FRAGRANCE

*How to Make
Natural Soaps, Scents
and Sundries*

1975   *New York*   ATHENEUM

The author wishes to express appreciation to E. J. Malchisky, Old Sturbridge Village, Sturbridge, Massachusetts, for permission to use the recipe for Rose Jar Mixture on page 25.

And to David Meyer, Indiana Botanic Gardens, Hammond, Indiana, for permission to quote from the Herbalist Almanac, *1965.*

DRAWINGS BY ROXANNE PLUMMER

To our sweet-smelling E A R T H —
may it survive the foolishness of man

CONTENTS

Color, and How to Get It *156*

FRAGRANCE

How to Make Natural Soaps,
Scents and Sundries

THE SENSUOUS
HOUSEHOLD

*S*OMETIMES AT our house, when I've served a mediocre kind of meal and haven't bothered to make a dessert, we play a game in which we all describe in detail what we'd order for dessert if we could have anything in the world we wanted. It's surprising how involved people get in playing the game and what strange and wonderful desserts are described. Once, when my seventy-eight-year-old father was visiting us, he waited his turn and then said thoughtfully, "If I could have any dessert I wanted I'd start out with two slices of white bread. I'd get me a big bowl and I'd tear that bread into chunks and I'd put it in the bowl. Then I'd pour squirrel gravy all over it." He paused and added, "Any man that don't like squirrel gravy, well, he don't know what's good for his pleasure."

A lot of people don't seem to know what's good for

their pleasure—even when it's available in a simple, easy-to-capture form. I've always felt it regrettable that people didn't take more pleasure in using their sense of smell. There are so many little ways to utilize this least developed of our senses.

In the long-gone days before people knew about bottled disinfectants and pressurized spray cans, they came up with some wonderfully inventive ways to pleasure their olfactory senses. They planted their walkways with thyme and sage, so that when people walked along, their boots crushed the plants and sent fragrance swimming into the air. The floors of their houses were covered ankle deep with sweet flag, woodruff, and Santolina—all gathered from the countryside. They offered their guests bowls of scented clay to wash away the dust of travel and a bowl of rose water for a fragrant rinse. Their clothes would be hung over a charcoal brazier sprinkled with frankincense, myrrh, and storax so the next time they put them on they smelled heavenly. When guests went off to sleep, their bed linens, already smelling of lavender, would have been sprinkled with spikenard, thyme, and even a grain or two of civet. Then, if they were not already too intoxicated with fragrance, they would be offered bed pillows stuffed with hops, because the fragrance of hops could bring a sweet, untroubled sleep. (If guests hoped for more interesting dreams, or even frightening ones, they could choose a pillow stuffed with mugwort.) Bedside candles would be flower scented, and the fireplace would hold the last fragrant embers of the roots of the juniper tree.

There is no way to completely duplicate such a fragrant household today, but the herbs, weeds, roots, and blossoms used in those long-gone times are still available, and many of the old practices can be adapted for today's use. Some of the following ideas are ones I've already tried, while others have to wait their turn on my list of things-to-do-when-there's-time.

Using Plants for Fragrance

Many plants, weeds included, can be ignited to take advantage of their fragrant parts. I hope no one would deliberately destroy a tree or shrub just to burn it, though. The idea is to use only those parts which are already dead or the spare parts left over after the plant has been put to some useful purpose. The following list describes a few fragrant plants and the ways they've been used. Some of them can be gathered from the countryside; others can be grown from seeds or cuttings. In instances where you might need specific scientific names in order to identify a plant, I've included them.

PLANTS TO BURN

DEERTONGUE OR WILD VANILLA (*Trilisa odoratissima*)

An herb that was dried, tied into bunches, and then burned to fumigate sickrooms and simply to impart fragrance. It has a mild, sweet, vanilla scent that makes it popular for potpourri mixes and for pipe tobacco mixes.

SPANISH IRIS OR ORRISROOT (*Iris florentina*)

Historically, the roots of this plant were dried and then burned for fragrance. It grows semiwild all over the South. The flowers are a lovely pale blue on slender stalks

spanish iris

about 18 inches long. The roots are used today in the manufacture of perfumes, dental preparations, and cosmetics.

ROSEMARY (*Rosemarinus officinalis*)

Rosemary is a favorite with everyone who grows or knows about herbs. It's fragrant when it's green or dried, and even without touching it, it exudes a clean pleasant smell. In addition to its fragrance, rosemary has germicidal properties that make it useful for sweetening the air and to "correct noxious, filthy smells." (There are many places I know about today that could profit from such a use!)

SCOTCH PINE

The roots of many pine trees are fragrant, but this one especially so. It also makes a lovely light.

rosemary

Juniper

Twigs, branches, and roots of many species of the juniper tree have been burned for both light and fragrance.

Elecampane or Elfwart (*Inula helenium*)

This beautiful weed with spectacular large, yellow flowers grows along shaded roadsides and in slightly damp meadows. Because the blossom is shaped like the rays of the sun, it was often used in the center of an herbal bouquet. The fragrant roots are strangely shaped, somewhat like a child's wooden top. They are cut and dried and burned for fragrance.

Elecampane

mullein

GREAT MULLEIN (*Verbascum thapsus*)

The tallest, proudest, sassiest-looking weed along country roads is probably the great mullein. It is a sturdy, stout-hearted fellow that reaches heights of 6 to 7 feet. The leaves, all clustered at the bottom, are velvety and whitish green, while a flower cluster at the top is pale yellow. Once called hag's taper, the stem and blossom were dried, soaked in oil, and then burned for light and fragrance.

RUSHES

There are large numbers of rushes that grow wild in almost every part of the United States. Most of them are grassy in appearance, with a slender, straight stalk surrounded by tapered leaves. One member of the rush

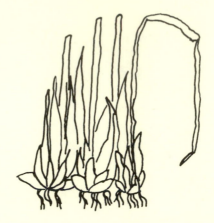

Juncus Effusus

family (*Juncus effusus*) was used by families in colonial America to give light to the cabins. The rushes were gathered by the children, hung to dry, and then stripped of the outer leaves. The slender stem was then dipped in tallow and set into a rush-light holder, where it would burn for about an hour. The holders for these rushes are collector's items today, and excellent examples can be seen in most Americana collections.

In making experiments with various rushes myself, I hit upon an interesting use for slender cattails, which can also be found growing wild. These small cattails (*Typha latifolia*) have a blossom end that is about five inches long and only a quarter of an inch in diameter. When the blossom end is ignited it burns slowly and evenly, turning inward as it burns like a curling baby's finger.

The natural woody fragrance of cattails is too slight to notice, so I perfume them by soaking the furred end

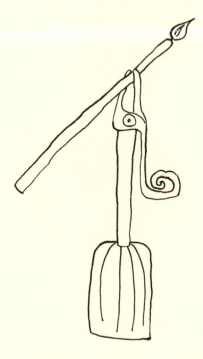

Rushlight holder

overnight in cologne or in an essential oil. After they dry, they are burned by setting them in a tall container of sand. They stop burning, conveniently, when they reach the spot where the blossom joins the stem.

LAVENDER (*Lavandula vera* and *Lavandula spica*)
Depending on the species, lavender grows in a slender spike from one to three feet tall. It's an especially gratifying plant—beautiful as it grows and fragrant in all its

parts. It grows even more fragrant after it dries. Lavender was gathered, dried, and then burned to fill rooms with fragrance.

STREWING HERBS

In old England, the floors of castles, cottages, and churches were often constructed of dirt or of stones. It was the custom then to lay down a thick carpet of herbs, rushes, or flowers to eliminate the task of sweeping and to dispel musty odors. It was also a good way to impress visiting dignitaries or friends. The poor folk had to use common germander or hyssop, while kings and queens could call for the strewing of flowers and blossoms or the stems and leaves of sweet flag. As people walked about, crushing the plants, the air was filled with fragrance. It seems such a delightful custom that I'd like to find a way to adopt it today. I'm not suggesting a return to dirt floors, but maybe we can find a way to incorporate strewing herbs into our households. I know at least one person who's done it. She puts lengths of fresh lavender under her door mat. Following is a list of the herbs most commonly used for strewing. All of these can be grown in the garden or can be purchased.

Balm	Hyssop	Rosemary
Basil	Lavender	Sage
Chamomile	Meadowsweet	Santolina
Costmary	Mint	Thyme
	Rue	

LAVENDER BALLS

In her book, *Herbs, Their Culture and Use*, Rosetta Clarkson describes a number of interesting ways to use lavender. She describes lavender-filled pads for scenting linens and for padding coat hangers. She even suggests attaching lavender sprigs to Christmas cards. But I was fascinated by her description of fans made from lavender stalks. She cut the stalks into identical lengths and laid them out on fan-shaped pieces of organdy fabric. They were covered by another layer of organdy and then stitched in place by rows of lavender-colored silk thread.

A different kind of use can be made of lavender stalks by weaving them into beautiful spheres reminiscent of the catnip balls children used to make. These spheres can be hung around the room, both to look pretty and to scent it.

When lavender has bloomed, cut an uneven number of stalks—either 9 or 11. Trim them off at the root end so they're all the same length, then remove the leaves so the stem is clear. Now tie a cord around the bunch, just below the flower heads. Carefully bend all the stems back

lavender ball

up and over the flowers and tie them together at the top. (This makes a cagelike ball, with the deep purple flowers in the center.)

Take a length of narrow ribbon, and starting at the bottom of the ball, weave in and out of the stems, going around the ball until you reach the halfway point. Cut the ribbon and secure it, then cut another length of ribbon and attach to the top of the ball so it can be suspended.

These will need to be made in the fall, when the flowers are in bloom. If you want to save them for Christmas gifts, put them into closed boxes to preserve their scent.

TUSSIE-MUSSIES AND BOUQUETS

Pretty young girls in Victorian portraits often clutched miniature bouquets backed by lacelike fans. Those bouquets were probably "tussie-mussies," and may not have been flowers at all but fragrant herbs. It was a common practice to make nosegays (something pretty for the nose) to take to sick friends or as small remembrances.

To make something pretty for your nose, or someone else's nose, gather herbs and flowers while they are fresh and tie them into a white paper doily. To do a really authentic number, try to find some elecampane (*Inula helenium*) for the center. Its color and shape were symbolic of the sun's rays, and were meant to bring warmth and health to the holder.

After you make a selection of herbs and flowers, tie them into a close little bunch. Cut a white lace paper doily down one side, wrap it around the base of the bouquet, and tie with a ribbon.

If you have hospitalized friends, you might find that they appreciate a nosegay rather than a bouquet of flowers. The herbs are fragrant without being overpowering, and best of all they don't have any sickroom overtones. Choose any fragrant herb, but note that, if you include rosemary, you will be saying, "Please remember me." A forget-me-not will say, "I love you." Heather means "I admire you." Sage denotes esteem. (Esteem is not to be

scorned!) Borage cheers the heart. And thyme, my favorite, lets you commune with the fairies.

If you wish to set out bowls of cut herbs for color and fragrance rather than tie them into a nosegay, you can choose from the following list:

Artemisia	Calendula	Mint
Basil	Clary sage	Rosemary
Bee balm	Costmary	Scented geranium leaves
Borage	Lavender	Sweet woodruff
	Marjoram	

PILLOWS

Herbs have been used to stuff both mattresses and pillows. Sweet woodruff was a favorite, as were agrimony and rosemary. There was more than perfume involved in the use of these herbs for stuffings. Rosemary, for instance, was used to cure a headache or to induce sleep. Sprigs were also placed under children's pillows to keep them from having bad dreams.

Though many herbal recipes and customs were left in the old country when settlers came to America, the practice of making herbal pillows survived, and was still in evidence during the Victorian era.

To make herbal pillows, keep in mind the way they're going to be used. Since they'll be used on the bed, and under your head, you'll want them to be soft and flat. You can take two handkerchiefs, sew them up on three sides to make an envelope, and then fill with about 4 to 6 ounces of herbs. Stitch the fourth side by hand. When the herbs have lost their fragrance, more can be added. The pillows should be rubbed and stroked and fluffed just before they're put to use. A few drops of water sprinkled on the pillow will lessen the crispy sound.

See the list below for pillow ingredients and their possibilities.

To induce sleep, try:

Lemon balm	Flowers of the hop plant
Cowslip	Mignonette

To calm nerves, try:

Chamomile	Sweet woodruff
Hyssop	Violet leaves and flowers
Cowslip	Chervil

To lift the spirit, try:

Sweet cicely	Heather
Any of the mints	Chervil

To cure a headache, try:

Lavender	Cowslip
Chamomile	Rosemary

To keep away evil spirits:

Rosemary

To invite trouble:

Mugwort

I put mugwort at the end because this herb can not only keep people from sleeping, it can take their minds to places they've never been before. If you would like to send out for a fantasy, try mugwort.

Plants to Grow for Fragrance

With the help of horticulturists from Old Sturbridge Village, the Missouri Botanical Gardens, Woodland Acres, Gardens of the Blue Ridge, Three Laurels, and

Leslie's Wildflower Nursery, I've assembled a list of plants that can be grown for their fragrance. Addresses of those institutions which can supply seeds or plants can be found in the back of the book. The list is divided into three parts: wildflowers, plants to grow outside, and plants that will grow inside.

WILDFLOWERS AND PLANTS FOR OUTDOOR GARDENS

Bee balm (Monarda Mahogany Red)
Bergamot (Monarda Purple)
Bugbane (*Cimicifuga americana*)
Butterfly weed (*Asclepias tuberosa*)
Fairybells (*Collinsonia canadensis*)
Lily of the valley (*Convallaria majalis*)
Marsh orchid (*Spirantha cernua*)
Oswego beebalm (*Monarda didyma*)
Red trillium (*Trillium sessile*)
Small purple fringed orchids (*Habenaria psycodes*)
Speckled clintonia (*Clintonea umbellata*)
Squirrel corn (*Dicentra canadensis*)
Sweet scented shrub (*Calycanthus floridus*)
Tansy (*Tanacetum* sp.)
Trailing arbutus (*Epigaea repens*)
Wild ginger (*Asarum canadense*)

INDOOR PLANTS

Airy lace geranium (*Pelargonium radens*)
Gardenia (*Gardenia jasminiodes*)
Lavender (*Lavendula*—all varieties)
Lily of the valley (*Convallaria majalis*)
Peppermint geranium (*Pelargonium tomentosum*)

Persian lime (*Citrus aurantifolia*)
Rosemary (all varieties)
Scented leaf geraniums (all varieties, including pep-
    permint, above, and lemon, lime, rose and oakleaf)
Sweet olive (*Osmanthas fragrans*)
Thyme (all varieties)
Wax plant (*Hoya carnosa variegata*)

Nearly all members of the citrus family are fragrant
also.

OUTDOOR PLANTS (A SELECTED LIST FROM OLD STURBRIDGE VILLAGE)

Peony (*Paeonia* hybrids)
Garden heliotrope (*Valeriana officinalis*)
Hyssop (*Hyssopus officinalis*)
Lemon verbena (*Lippia citriodora*)
German chamomile (*Matricaria chamomilla*)
Mints (*Mentha*, including apple, peppermint,
    spearmint, lemon)
Pineapple sage (*Salvia rutilans*)
Bee balm (*Monarda didyma*)
Lemon balm (*Melissa officinalis*)
Ambrosia (*Chenopodium ambrosoides*)
Thyme (all varieties)
Lavender (*Lavandula vera*)
Lily of the valley (*Convallaria majalis*)
Sweet marjoram (*Marjorana hortensis*)
Mignonette (*Reseda odorata*)
Rosemary (*Rosmarinus officinalis*)
Lavender cotton (*Santolina chamaecyperus*)
Roman wormwood (*Artemisia absinthium*)
Southernwood (*Artemisia abrotanum*)

Tarragon (*Artemisia dracunculus*)
Clove pink (*Dianthus caryophyllus*)
Sweet woodruff (*Asperula odorata*)
Tansy (*Tanacetum vulgare*)
Violet (*Viola odorata*)
Feverfew (*Chrysanthemum parthenium*)

Potpourris and Sachets

Potpourris and sachets are mixtures of dried, fragrant plant materials. The foliage and blossoms are both used; the flowers, however, are used mainly for color. Both sachets and potpourris have the same function—to give off a clean, natural scent. In very broad general terms, potpourri mixtures are whole or cut, while those of the sachet are chopped, ground, and powdered. Some people add essential oils to the mixtures; other abhor the thought of doing such a thing. I see no harm in it myself. The other difference between the two mixtures is that sachets are usually tucked out of sight in drawers, closets, and so on, while a potpourri is meant to be viewed.

GATHERING AND PREPARING
POTPOURRI MATERIALS

If you have access to fragrant materials, you'll be collecting ingredients all summer long as plants blossom and mature. Gather the plants early in the morning while they're still fresh. Shake away the morning dew and lay out on drying racks or screens. (You can use an old window screen, elevated away from the ground so air can circulate.) If it's a breezy day, cover the screen with cheesecloth. Take the plants in each evening.

If you have drying space indoors, you can do the job there rather than set up outside each day. It's a less troublesome procedure. Set out on trays; the plants should be turned occasionally.

As the materials dry—they should be crackling dry— store them in dry, airtight boxes or jars, being sure to label them. Keep away from the light to preserve colors. Maintain a separate container for decorative materials— the petals, blossoms, or buds—that you will want for color and beauty.

See "Gathering and Extracting the Fragrance of Plants" (pages 145–155) for more details on gathering and preparing.

When all the materials you've gathered are ready to mix, collect them in one place, along with containers for storage. Before the plants are put into final potpourri jars, they will be mixed and blended for a 6- to 8-week period. So at this time you want large containers that need only to be practical, not beautiful. An old canister set is good. The important thing to remember is that the storage container should provide dry, light-tight storage.

You will also want to have a fixative on hand, plus spices and essential oils. (See the list of fixatives, spices, and plants that follows.)

Following one of the ensuing recipes, or one of your own, pour the ingredients into a flat enamel or glass pan. For every quart of dry material, add 1 tablespoon of fixative. Next, add the spices, citrus rind, essential oils, and so on. Stir with a light hand, then store to age and blend fragrances, stirring occasionally as the blend progresses.

At the end of the 6-week aging period, bring out the

mixture and put into beautiful, see-through glass containers. (If it's a sachet, it will be sewn into fabric enclosures.) Add the decorative materials to the mixture as you put it in the jars.

SCENTED PLANT MATERIAL FOR POTPOURRIS AND SACHETS

This is a partial list of fragrant materials. Since there are hundreds of plants that are fragrant when dried, this list will get you started—you can progress from there if you like.

Acacia	Mint
Basil	Orange tree (leaves)
Calamus (root)	Patchouli
Cassia buds	Rose
Lavender	Rose geranium (leaves)
Lemon balm	Rosemary
Lemon thyme	Sandalwood (bark)
Lemon tree (leaves)	Sweet lemongrass
Lemon verbena	Violet
Marjoram	White oak (bark)

SPICES AND MISCELLANEOUS

Aniseed	Mace
Allspice	Nutmeg (coarsely ground)
Caraway seeds	Vanilla bean
Cinnamon sticks	Crushed, dried peel of lemon,
Cloves	lime, orange, grapefruit
Coriander seeds	Assorted essential oils

BLOSSOMS FOR COLOR AND FORM

Bee balm	Marigold
Carnation	Nasturtium
Crab apple	Orange blossom
Delphinium	Pansy
Honeysuckle	Pink
Larkspur	Rose (petals and buds)
Lavender	Strawflower
Lilac	Violet

FIXATIVES

The function of the fixative is to hold and blend other scents. Fixatives can be either of plant or animal origin. Animal fixatives are ambergris, civet, and musk. Some plant fixatives are gum benzoin, clary sage leaves, orris-root, oakmoss, and tonka beans.

Note: Fixatives should be powdered for sachets and whole or cut for potpourris.

POTPOURRIS
GRANDMOTHER'S GARDEN POTPOURRI
    1 pint rosemary leaves
    1 pint lavender leaves and flowers
    1 tablespoon orrisroot (cut)
    Optional essential oil: 2 drops oil of rose geranium

NEW MORNING POTPOURRI
    1 cup rose petals
    1 cup orange blossoms

1 cup sweet lemongrass
1 cup lemon thyme
1 tablespoon aniseed (crushed)
1 tablespoon caraway seeds (crushed)
1 tablespoon tonka beans (crushed) or orrisroot (cut)

LAVENDER POTPOURRI I

2 cups lavender flowers and leaves
2 cups rose leaves and petals
¼ cup cloves (bruised)
¼ cup cinnamon sticks (broken)
2 tablespoons gum benzoin (cut)

LAVENDER POTPOURRI II

2 cups lavender flowers and leaves
2 cups rose petals and leaves
2 tablespoons cinnamon sticks (broken)
2 tablespoons cloves (bruised)
2 tablespoons gum benzoin (cut)
6 drops of each:
    oil of lavender
    oil of sandalwood
    oil of rose geranium
    oil of bergamot
    oil of lemon
Optional: 2 tablespoons tonka beans (crushed)
Optional essential oil: 10 drops tincture of musk

CITRUS POTPOURRI

2 cups mixed citrus rinds (crushed)
1 cup lemon balm
1 cup lemon thyme

2 tablespoons coriander seeds (bruised)
1 dropper (20 to 24 drops) oil of lemon
1 dropper (20 to 24 drops) oil of orange
10 drops oil of bergamot
1 tablespoon orrisroot (powdered)

ROSE JAR MIXTURE (Courtesy Old Sturbridge Village)
1 quart rose petals (dried)
1 tablespoon orrisroot (cut)
1 tablespoon mixed nutmeg, cinnamon, and allspice (crushed)
1 tablespoon gum benzoin

Mix the above ingredients in a pottery bowl. When well mixed, add bits of vetiver root, vanilla bean, dried orange peel stuck with clove.

Divide the mixture into thirds. Put one-third in a rose jar, then add a few drops rose oil, oil of rosemary, and lemon verbena. Add another third, repeat the oils. Do this until the jar is filled. Seal for 6 weeks, then break the seal and stir well with wooden spoon. Each season, add more rose petals, keeping the jar filled.

SACHETS

During the 1890s, sachet making was considered to be a part of the growing-up ritual for young girls—almost like a puberty rite. Young girls sat down with baskets of ribbons, satin, lace, and velvet and turned out sachets by the score. They were tucked into any space that would hold them—drawers where lingerie was stored, linen closets, in the folds of couches or armchairs, and among the books on library shelves. Some were even pinned to

sachets

draperies, where the warmth of the sun could set their fragrance free.

To make a sachet today, choose a lightweight fabric which has a design and color to fit the contents. I like to use calico for an old-fashioned spicy scent. Yellow satin fits an exotic mix. Lavender voile or gauze is nice for flowered scents.

Cut the fabric into 4-inch squares and sew it up on three sides. Turn right side out and stuff with the sachet material. Stitch the fourth side by hand, with invisible stitches. Decorate with abandon, and attach a ribbon if it's to be hung in the closet.

Follow the directions for making potpourris, using any of the potpourri recipes on pages 23–25, or select one of the following.

LIGHTLY SCENTED SACHET
    2 cups crushed chamomile flowers
    1 cup orrisroot (cut)

HEAVILY SCENTED SACHET
    2 cups patchouli leaves
    ½ cup sandalwood (powdered)
    2 drops oil of rose geranium

FOREST SACHET
    1 cup rose leaves
    ½ cup sandalwood (powdered)
    2 drops oil of rose geranium

LEMON SACHET
    2 cups lemon or orange peel (dried and cut into bits—
        you can use the blender)
    1 tablespoon caraway seeds (bruised)
    1 tablespoon coriander seeds (bruised)
    2 tablespoons ambrette seeds (bruised)

MY FAVORITE SACHET
    ½ cup rose leaves
    1 cup lavender flowers
    1 cup calamus root (cut)
    1 tablespoon coriander seeds (bruised)
    1 tablespoon orrisroot (powdered)
    2 drops oil of rhodium
    4 drops tincture of musk

POWDERED VIOLET SACHET—EXTRA NICE
    2 cups violet roots (powdered)
    2 tablespoons sandalwood (powdered)
    1 drop oil of orange
    1 drop oil of lemon
    1 drop oil of sandalwood
    6 drops tincture of musk
    2 drops tincture of civet

LAVENDER SACHET
>   2 cups lavender leaves and flowers
>   1 tablespoon gum benzoin (powdered)
>   2 drops oil of lavender

MUSK-ORANGE SACHET
>   1 cup orange peel (dried, cut, and bruised in
>   blender)
>   ½ cup orrisroot (cut)
>   2 tablespoons tonka beans (cut)
>   6 drops tincture of musk
>   3 drops oil of sandalwood

FINELY POWDERED SACHET

Nice for a man's socks and underwear drawers. A very old cookbook described this as being "an acceptable present to a single gentleman."

>   ½ cup cornstarch
>   1 tablespoon orrisroot (powdered)
>   5 drops oil of lemon
>   2 drops oil of lavender
>   2 drops tincture of musk

Beads, Pomanders, and Other Organic Jewelry

In early England, men and women wore jewelry made of scented gums. It was a good idea in those days to carry good scents with you in as many ways as you could find to do it. Roomfuls of people who seldom bathed, would, I imagine, create a very unmanageable odor. And of course people knew that many herbs and gums contained germicidal qualities that could be used to prevent infection from disease. As a common practice, then, traveling salesmen carried fragrant gums into the countryside where housewives shaped them into simple necklaces and bracelets. Some of the gums were mixed with herbs, honey, spices, and so on, and rolled into beads or balls. Or they were made into pastes and put into tiny boxes called "cassolettes." These boxes were usually made of precious metal with perforated lids, and when refreshment was needed, they could be discreetly brought out and the scent inhaled. Some mixtures were even stuffed inside the head of a man's cane.

The most elaborate form of organic jewelry, though, was the pomander. Originally designed to be carried to ward off infection and to subdue unpleasant odors, they soon became an excuse for the creation of exquisite pieces of jewelry. Hollow gold or silver balls were created to be filled with fragrant gums and spices. They either hung from the neck or dangled from the belt, where they could be reached in a hurry.

As personal cleanliness became more commonplace, pomanders were taken off the body and changed from pieces of jewelry to room ornaments. These pomanders were often made of china, richly decorated, and they were filled with fragrant mixtures and hung around the room.

A TWENTIETH-CENTURY POMANDER

To make a mixture to use in a china pomander ball, use any of the potpourri recipes on pages 23–25. Or try one of my favorites: a mixture of equal parts of sandalwood, rue, and rose petals, plus a dropper (20 to 24 drops) tincture of ambergris. Or, equal parts of ground orange peel, lavender flowers, and rose petals, plus a dropper oil of orange and a dropper oil of jasmine.

China pomander balls are sold in gift shops and stores that sell bath supplies.

Sometimes, instead of using a china ball, I make a hanging container from a small gourd. I saw off the top, perforate it with a drill and then fill the ball with scented material. The top is then glued back on or attached with decorative cord, and the gourd suspended from the ceiling.

FRUIT POMANDER

Many of the pomanders we see today are made with oranges as a base, but they can also be made of apples, lemons, or limes. Choose a fresh, firm piece of fruit and gather the following dry ingredients:

> 2 teaspoons cloves (powdered)
> 2 teaspoons cinnamon (powdered)
> 2 teaspoons allspice
> 4 teaspoons orrisroot (powdered)
> Also, have on hand 1 box of whole cloves

Place the dry ingredients (except whole cloves) in a bowl and stir to mix.

Using an ice pick or sharp skewer completely cover the body of the fruit with holes. (The holes are for the insertion of the cloves.)

To make a hanger, thread a long needle (a mattress

needle 6 to 8 inches long is a good tool) with carpeting thread. Take the thread down through the fruit from the top and out through the bottom. Come back up through the fruit ½ inch away from the first hole. Join the thread in a loop about 6 inches long and tie with a knot.

Press 1 clove into each of the holes (stem first) until the fruit is completely covered. When completely covered, roll in the bowl of dried ingredients, letting the fruit soak up as much as it can absorb.

Put it away, now, in a clean, dry place to allow it to mellow. It will eventually become dry and quite light. Decorate it with yarn or ribbon and it can be hung in the closet to do its thing.

MYRRH BEADS

These beads will give off a musky exciting fragrance. In the time of Jesus, myrrh was tied into a cloth bag and worn so it hung between the breasts. The warmth of the skin released the fragrance.

I make myrrh beads about the size of a small plum and then place them between two interesting buttons. They are mottled shades of brown, cream and white; the fragrance seems to be eternal. This recipe makes 4 beads.

    3 teaspoons gum myrrh (cut)
    1 ½ teaspoons gum benzoin (powdered)
    1 ½ teaspoons liquid storax
    3 heaping tablespoons beeswax chips or slivers of paraffin

Place the first three ingredients together in a bowl while melting the wax over hot water. Then pour the melted wax over the ingredients in the bowl, mixing until well blended. Form into balls, then flatten each slightly on two sides so it will lie between 2 buttons. Pierce with a needle while still malleable and let dry for 48 hours.

String in whatever way pleases you. A thin leather thong, knotted at intervals, goes well with the character of the beads. Glass beads can be integrated into the necklace. When not in use, keep in a closed box, although the fragrance is very lasting.

AMBRETTE SEED NECKLACE

These pale brown, grainlike seeds give off an elusive fragrance—a combination of oranges and freshly bathed baby. Some people, including myself, string them as necklaces. Body warmth unlocks their scent.

Let a quantity of the seeds soak in a bowl of water for 2 to 4 hours to soften. One cupful makes an average-length necklace. Thread a needle with fine bead thread and string them alone or in combination with other materials. A spectacular combination can be made with glass or copper beads. Or add one of the following seeds for accent:

Star anise, a star-shaped woody seed that smells marvelous and brings good luck to the wearer.

Tonka beans, almond-shaped and black, they smell like fresh vanilla; they are love charms.

Jumbie seeds. Bean-sized crimson and black seeds, they have no fragrance, but they may drive away evil spirits.

Job's tears. Of an opalescent gray color, these have no fragrance either, but the combination of color and silky sheen make them soothing to touch. They serve some people as prayer beads.

ROSE BEADS

In my great-grandmother's time, children made beads from rose petals to give as gifts. The beads were sturdy and long lasting, and many of them were used as the beads in rosaries. The old recipes for rose beads seem extremely complicated. The following one is a simplified version.

> 1 handful rose petals (fresh or dried)
> 2 handfuls chamomile flowers and leaves (dried)

Place both ingredients in a glass or enamel saucepan and barely cover with water. Simmer 1 hour; do not boil. If the water level drops, add just enough to cover the petals. Remove from the heat and pour into a blender. Blend for 2 minutes, or until the mixture looks pulpy. Squeeze out excess moisture and roll into beads about the size of a marble. Set aside to dry.

When the beads have lost most of their moisture, thread a needle with bead thread and string them. Move them about on the string as they dry so they won't be irrevocably stuck in one spot, then hang to finish drying. When dry, move them together on the string and tie a knot in the ends to complete the necklace. Keep them in a closed drawer or box to preserve their scent.

These beads dry to a dark rosy brown, and smell delicious. They will be rough and tweedy looking. I like that—but their roughness can be subdued with a wood file, too.

Rose beads can also be strung with accent beads of glass or brass.

Incense from Plants and Gums

The perfumed smoke that rises from the burning of plants, gums, bark, and so on is called incense. It's quite inexpensive to buy, and therefore may not seem worth the effort to make. But it's very easy to do, and if you do make your own you can have fun experimenting with a large variety of scents from your own plants, oils, and so forth.

Traditionally, the burning of incense was connected to religious ceremonies. It was also used to some extent to drive away evil spirits or collect good ones. Now the primary purpose of most of the incense on the market is to add fragrant smoke to the air.

I'm very enthusiastic about handmade incense because of the wide variety of scents that are possible and because it makes such a beautiful gift. The ingredients are easy to find, and can be turned into leafy, powdered, or molded forms. The following recipes can serve as a starting point for experiments of your own.

MIXTURES FOR PAPER CONES

Dry, fragrant incense materials can be blended and stored in glass jars and then burned a pinch or two at a time. Whenever you want a brief but fragrant encounter, make a small paper cone, fill it with the dried material and then light the tip end.

To make a cone, cut out a paper triangle about 2½ inches at the widest part. Roll it into a cone. (I put one

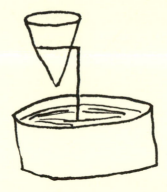

staple at the top to stabilize it.) Slip this one into a holder made by bending a paper clip into a S-shaped holder. Set the holder into a bowl of sand to burn and fill it with incense. Ignite the bottom end.

Sawdust to use in the following recipes can come from woodshop floors or from lumberyards. Sift it through an ordinary kitchen flour sifter; one time through makes it fine enough to burn.

When all the ingredients are mxied, they can be stored in pretty glass jars and kept handy. A jar of these materials makes a lovely gift.

Thyme Incense I
    2 tablespoons thyme (powdered)
    2 tablespoons sawdust

Thyme Incense II
    2 tablespoons thyme (powdered)
    2 tablespoons sandalwood chips
    2 tablespoons sawdust

Sandalwood Incense
    2 tablespoons sandalwood chips
    ¼ cup cinnamon (powdered)
    2 tablespoons sawdust

Rosemary Incense
    ¼ cup rosemary
    ¼ cup sawdust

Frankincense
    2 tablespoons sawdust
    1 teaspoon cinnamon (powdered)
    1 teaspoon cloves (powdered)
    2 tablespoons frankincense (powdered)

Patchouli Incense
    1 tablespoon gum benzoin (powdered)
    1 tablespoon sandalwood chips
    1 tablespoon patchouli leaves
    1 tablespoon aloe (There are several aloes. They're
      all fragrant.)
    2 tablespoons sawdust

Outdoorsy Incense
    2 tablespoons sawdust
    2 tablespoons ginger (powdered
    1 tablespoon nutmeg (powdered)

Other herbs to experiment with, alone or together:
lavender, sage, curry, lemon verbena, lavender flowers,
chamomile heads.

MOLDED INCENSE

The base for the following recipes is finely sifted sawdust. After aromatic materials are added, the sawdust is made into a "dough" by mixing it with a syrup of gum arabic. As in the previous recipes, I use ordinary sawdust gathered from woodshop floors or from lumberyards. The sawdust, of course, should be dry. I sift it twice through my kitchen flour sifter.

Basic Procedure

The basic procedure for all the recipes is the same. The recipe calls for 1 cup of sawdust, which will make up into 30 or 40 cylinders about 1½ inches long and ¼ inch in diameter. The recipe is easy to increase or decrease as you wish. Or the basic recipe can be divided after it is mixed and perfumed with different scenting materials.

For each cup of sawdust, make up a syrupy glue by adding 2⅔ tablespoons of powdered gum arabic to 1 cup of water. Stir until it is free of lumps.

Place the sawdust in a glass or stainless steel bowl and add your perfumed materials. Then add the syrup of gum arabic, a little at a time, until the mixture can be molded; It will feel grainy and somewhat sandy. Roll, pat, or fondle it into cylindrical shapes. They will look husky and dependable. Don't be afraid to add a bit more water if the dough seems dry, or more sawdust if you get it too wet.

Warning: This mix will not feel like bread dough. It will look at first as though it will not stick together. But once you get it in shape, it will stay that way. After it dries a bit so it can be handled, you can put a toothpick up inside the cylinder to act as a kind of stem. The cylinders need to dry 48 hours before they can be burned, and after drying they should be kept in a dry, closed container. Aging improves the fragrance.

Note in the recipes below that 1 dropper measures out to be about 20 to 24 drops.

Basic Incense Ingredients
　　1 cup sawdust
　　1 cup gum arabic syrup

Benzoin Incense I
　　A clean, woody smell. To the basic ingredients (above), add ¼ cup gum benzoin (powdered).

Benzoin Incense II
　　An added flower note over the woody smell. Add 6 droppers tincture of ambergris to Benzoin Incense I.

Sweet and Spicy Incense
　　This smells innocent and seductive at the same time. To the basic incense ingredients (above) add:
　　　　2 teaspoons storax (semiliquid)
　　　　¼ cup gum benzoin (powdered)
　　　　1 dropper oil of clove

Musk and Frankincense
　　A super fragrance! Smells fresh and flowerlike. To the basic incense ingredients (above) add:
　　　　6 tablespoons frankincense (powdered)
　　　　15 droppers tincture of musk
　　Note: This amount of musk may seem out of propor-

tion, but the musk in a tincture is delicate and requires a larger volume than if it were an oil.

Citrus Incense

A fresh, fruit fragrance. To the basic incense ingredients (above) add:

 6 tablespoons angelica root (powdered)
 8 droppers oil of orange
 8 droppers oil of lime
 12 droppers oil of lemon

Exotic Incense

An elegant fragrance, reminiscent of honey and wine. To the basic incense ingredients (above) add:

 ¼ cup gum benzoin (powdered)
 8 droppers tincture of ambergris
 8 droppers tincture of musk
 4 droppers tincture of civet

CHARCOAL TAB INCENSE

There are some handy little items for sale in perfumery shops, shops that sell to the witchcraft trade, or in those places that have come to be known as "head shops." Some gift shops sell them, too. These are packets of charcoal tabs about 1½ inches across and ½ inch deep. They're like little black thumbprints with a small depression in the middle. These tabs are self-igniting, which doesn't mean they'll burst into flame on their own, but that they will ignite immediately when a match is held to them. In order not to be startled the first time you light one, be advised that they sparkle. The sparkle goes all around the tab and then settles down to burn like charcoal burns, with an intense glow.

The tabs are unscented, which is where the fun comes in, for this gives you a chance to drop your own scented materials on them. The tab is placed in an incense burner, or in a bowl of sand and then ignited. After it begins to glow, you add pinches or drops of whatever you have on hand as a scenting material. A word of warning—charcoal gives off intense heat, so even when an incense burner is used, it should be placed in a position where it won't damage the surface under it. I like to place a layer of sand in the bottom of the burner for added safety purposes.

Check the following list for ideas about what to try on these nifty tabs. For a gift, you could give packages of the tabs and make up containers of your own incense concoctions to go with them.

SCENTING MATERIALS FOR TABS

Most of the scented gums are nice. Try balsam of tolu, storax, frankincense, myrrh, or benzoin, alone or in combination.

Animal tinctures such as ambergris or musk are nice. Don't try civet alone! It is overpowering.

The essential oils can all be used, or at least tried. They vary in strength, of course, and you may need to experiment with combinations to get what you really enjoy. The drops of oil burn up quickly, so if you use them you'll probably want to reinforce the tab several times.

Following is a list of dry materials I've used and enjoyed.

    Cloves (both whole and powdered)
    Nutmeg (powdered)

Rosemary leaves and stems
Rue
Sandalwood
Thyme
Myrrh (cut)
Sweet woodruff
Star anise and aniseed
Lavender
Angelica root

INCENSE PAPERS

Several different kinds of papers can be perfumed and treated so they will burn evenly. Among the papers I've tried are blotting paper, constuction paper, index card stock, and Japanese rice paper.

The papers are cut into strips and then soaked in a solution of saltpeter, essential oils, and water. The saltpeter, which is available in drugstores, is applied to assure an even burn.

To make incense papers, add 3 tablespoons saltpeter to 3 cups boiling water and stir to dissolve. Let this mixture cool, then add 1 dropper (20 to 24 drops) of the perfumed essential oil you've chosen for each ounce of solution. You can choose one oil or a combination of them.

In the meantime, cut paper into strips. (I make mine 5 inches long by 2 inches wide.) Drop these strips into the perfumed solution and soak for a few minutes—just long enough to wet the paper without making it soggy. Then hang the strips to dry. (I attach a paper clip to each one and then hook the clip over a string drawn from one side of the kitchen window to the other. They look like someone has done the laundry for tiny people with rectangular bodies.)

After the strips are dry, store them in a box with a tight-fitting lid.

To use, light one corner of the paper and then extinguish the flame; the paper will continue to smolder. Lay the paper in a bowl of sand. If you write a wish on the paper first, maybe the smoke will carry it up to heaven.

If, after a time, you want to add more fragrance to your papers, they can be dipped into essential oil again. Cologne can be used in place of the oils, if you like.

I should add that some papers have been treated with chemicals that have a smell of their own. It's not a bad smell, it's just not a good one. So you may have to experiment to find a paper you like. Blotting paper and rice paper seem to be neutral, and are good ones to start with.

JUST ONE MORE INCENSE THING

It's possible to buy unscented incense sticks from the same place you buy charcoal tabs—the idea being that you scent these sticks with your handmade scents. Before I started making my own sawdust forms for incense, I liked to use these with my own cologne and combinations of essential oils. They are quite reasonable in price, and allow you to use your own imagination plus your own handmade oils.

To scent them, you can apply the oil or cologne with an eye dropper, but I also like to stand the sticks in a slender bottle filled with perfume material. I leave them there overnight and then dry them.

BEAUTY
AND THE BATH

*B*ATHING HASN'T ALWAYS been a popular practice. In colonial America, for instance, bathing was about as popular as a toothache, and people got by by washing only separate parts of themselves, as the occasion demanded. But today everyone is expected to bathe if they're to be socially acceptable. Bathing, in fact, has become such a popular form of entertainment that a whole mystique has been built up around it. There are hundreds of bath products on the market, all of them designed to make the entertainment more spectacular. There are oils, gelées, creams, special sponges and scrubbers, splashes, and milks. And products that tingle, bubble, soothe, and smooth. Fortunately, a good many of these luxury items can be made at home with no more effort than it takes to brew a pot of coffee. And it's fun to give them as gifts, packaged in original kinds of containers.

Following are some recipes for you to try—most of them made with ordinary, down-home ingredients.

General Directions

Equipment—bowls, storage jars, and so forth—should be either stainless steel or glass.

You may want to keep a separate set of measuring spoons for making fragrant items. Some of the essential oils are super powerful, and cling an egregiously long time to whatever they have a chance to cling to. If you don't use separate utensils, rinse them immediately after use in hot water. Then wash and rinse in a solution of half vinegar and half water. Ammonia and water will work in the same proportions, too.

Soft or distilled water is best for bath products.

Eyedroppers are handy for measuring oils. They cost ten cents apiece at the drugstore. You can use a drinking straw, but it's not quite as handy. When a recipe calls for "one dropper," this is equivalent to 20 to 24 drops. Generally, when adding essential oils, the precise number of drops is not critical. An attempt should be made to be accurate, but there's no reason to be overwhelmed by measurements.

Since these recipes don't call for any of the commercial additives that prolong the shelf life of cosmetic products, it's best not to make up huge amounts of anything at one time. Some of them, too, will want to be kept in the refrigerator. Those will be pointed out in the text.

You will see that some recipes call for tincture of benzoin. This is a tincture made from natural benzoin. It not

only prolongs the life of creams, oils, and so on, but adds a special healing and soothing property to these products. Tincture of benzoin can be purchased from a druggist. You may add 6 drops to every 4 ounces of fat or oil in the recipe.

Bath products can make beautiful gifts, especially if you package them in interesting containers. Old pickle jars, steak sauce bottles, cigar humidors, small cheese crocks, and wine bottles are some examples of what you can use.

Just as you may be allergic to some foods, you may also be allergic to some of the ingredients in these recipes. You probably don't need to be reminded, but I'll do it any-

way, that these recipes provide products that are meant
for the outside of the body, not the inside.

Herbal Teas for the Bath

Herbs, or combinations of them, have been used for centuries. At one time, in fact, they were the only form of
medicine and the only material available to create scents.
Depending on their special properties, they were used to
soothe or tone muscles, to ease tired minds, to take away
an itch, or just to make people feel beautiful.

Bathing in a tub of water juiced with herbs can be an
almost mystical experience. There are hundreds of herbs
and probably thousands of combinations that can be made
of them, so the recipes here are only a small taste of what
the total possibilities are. The following are ones I've
made and enjoyed myself.

There are two methods for using the herbal baths you
prepare. One is to mix the dried herbs and then tie them
up in a square of cloth about 5 x 5 inches. The bag is then
hung over the hot water faucet, where the water will
pass through it. The bag can also be dropped directly
into the tub along with your body, and stay there during
the bath. (Herbs floating free can clog up the drain, so be
sure to keep them captive.) If you want to make up bags
of herbs to give away, use different colored fabrics to act
as a key to the contents. A red striped fabric can indicate
a spicy mixture. Yellow can be used for a calming chamomile brew.

The second method of using herbal teas is to simmer
the herbs for 5 minutes, steep them for 10, and then pour
the mixture directly into the tub through a strainer. This

method is much more satisfactory than the first. The "tea" is stronger and does a better job, plus the fact that the fragrance created by simmering the tea is a beautiful bonus.

Some recipes are followed by a suggestion for a complementary essential oil. Essential oils are perfume oils available from druggists, herbalists, and many gift shops. The oil should be added after the herbs are simmered.

Mint Cooler

Fragrant and cooling. A good mixture for a hot day.

Mix equal parts of peppermint leaves, pine needles, and alfalfa mint leaves.

Complementary oil: add 1 dropper oil of rosemary or oil of bergamot to a quart of dry material.

Sweet Bath

A partially wholesome, partially sensuous combination—for people who want a little of both worlds.

½ cup sweet woodruff
½ cup sweet cicely
¼ cup angelica leaves
¼ cup hyssop leaves
¼ cup patchouli leaves

Complementary oil: 1 dropper oil of bergamot or 4 drops oil of patchouli.

Lemon Cooler

Good to make ahead and have on hand for summer afternoons.

1 cup lemon verbena
1 cup lemon balm
1 cup cowslip flowers

Complementary oil: 1 dropper oil of orange plus 1 dropper oil of lemon.

A Bath for Tired, Strained Muscles

The leaves of the bay plant (the same bay leaves that go into stews) have always been a favorite remedy for tired muscles. I don't know if it's my imagination or not, but a bath in bay really does perk me up when I'm tired. The leaves are especially fragrant. This is one herb tea I feel should be used only after it is simmered, so the best qualities of the herb will come through.

Simmer ½ cup bay leaves in 2 cups water for 5 minutes. Steep for 10 and strain directly into a hot bath.

Winter Warmer

One of my favorite baths. It's very fragrant—almost heady.

Simmer ½ cup white oak bark in 2 cups water for 5 minutes. Strain and pour directly into the tub.

Rosy Bath for a Cloudy Day

Spicy and sweet—a good mixture for gifts. Place in calico bags and tie with green ribbon.

    1 cup rose geranium leaves
    1 cup blackberry leaves
    1 cup elder flowers

Complementary oil: 1 dropper rose oil compound or 1 dropper rose geranium.

Invigorating Bath

Hyssop is an herb used for its ability to relieve skin irritations. Its leaves promote healing, and its fumes are touted as a brain medicine. It has a minty fragrance.

1 cup hyssop leaves
¾ cup lemon balm
Complementary oil: 4 drops oil of rosemary.

A SOAK FOR WEARY FEET

Lady's bedstraw is a versatile herb. It's been used to stuff mattresses, to make dye, and to curdle milk in the cheesemaking process. Made into a warm foot bath, it has a soothing effect on muscles and ligaments.

Simmer 1 handful in 2 cups water for 5 minutes. Strain into a foot basin of warm water and let your feet soak while you read a good book.

A SUPER FOOT BATH

This will make all twenty-six of your foot bones feel pampered. They deserve pampering now and then, considering how much hard work they do.

This recipe requires extra energy to prepare, but it's an elegantly satisfying ceremony. Prepare one for a friend or lover.

Get together:

1 cup rosemary leaves
1 cup table salt

Have two basins ready, each of them large enough for a pair of feet. First prepare a tea by simmering the rosemary in a pint of water for 5 minutes. Pour the tea, after it has cooled, into one basin containing enough cold water to cover the feet. Fill the other basin with water as hot as you can stand. Stir the cup of salt into the hot water.

Soak your feet in the hot salt bath for 5 minutes, then dip them into the rosemary bath for just one minute. Back into the hot bath for another 5 minutes, and then dip once more into the rosemary. Now after one last time in the salty mixture, scrub the feet with a brush to get rid of flaky unwanted skin and then rinse in rosemary as a final rinse. Your feet will feel like they've just won a million dollars. For a grand super finale, pour a few drops oil of rosemary into the palm of your hands and rub your feet with this. Rosemary has antiseptic properties, and will also make your feet smell a lot like a pine forest.

A FOOT BATH FOR PEOPLE WHO ARE
SELF-CONSCIOUS ABOUT FOOT SMELLS

This is a deodorizing and toning bath that requires a large amount of dedication. It smells wonderful, but I've no idea at all how long it keeps the feet odor free. I guess I never wanted to take off my shoes periodically to check on its efficacy. These leaves and berries can be used in either the cut or powdered form. I prefer using the cut form.

½ cup pennyroyal
½ cup sage
½ cup rosemary
½ cup angelica
½ cup juniper berries

Make a tea by placing the above ingredients in a pan containing 1 quart of water. Bring to a boil, then reduce the heat and simmer for 5 minutes. Cover and steep for another 10 minutes, then bottle for use. You can strain it, but I like to leave the herbs in. Use it in warm water, 1 cup for each foot bath.

Herbal Sauna Vapors

There is a point during a sauna bath (at least in saunas where a wood fire is used) when it's desirable to throw a cupful of water onto the stones to create steam. Instead using plain water, you can use an herbal tea to add fragrance to the room. It gives a sensational effect.

To make the tea, use any of the preceding recipes for herbal teas. One cupful is nice, but another cupful later on is even nicer. Following are several special vapor recipes, but you might want to try others, too.

Remember that herbs have real medicinal properties and therefore shouldn't be considered benign. Some of them, as you no doubt know from reading history, have been used to do away with enemies. So before you use an unknown herb (for any purpose), check to see what its properties are.

VAPORS OF NEW-MOWN HAY

Sweet woodruff smells as nice as its name implies. Angelica was once used for its antiwitchcraft powers.

½ cup sweet woodruff leaves
½ cup angelica root (either powdered or cut)
1 quart water

Make a tea according to directions for bath teas (page 48).

RAINY FOREST VAPORS

Oak has a sweet woody odor that is enlivened by cedarwood.

1 cup white oak bark
½ cup cedarwood chips
1 quart water

Make into tea as above.

yarrow

LAVENDER MIST

A delicate mind-soother—my favorite. It even gets rid
of headaches.

    1 cup lavender flowers

    ½ cup rose geranium leaves

    ½ cup patchouli leaves

    1 quart water

Make into a tea as above.

Following are some herbs you can try for sauna vapors.
Use them alone or in combination with others.

    Blackberry leaves

    Chamomile flowers and foliage

    Horsetail grass

    Lovage root

    Peppermint leaves

    Sage leaves

    Yarrow

    Vetiver root

Soaks

The following soaks are made from ordinary household products. They give an immense amount of pleasure and can also make impressively handsome gifts. They keep well and can be packaged in attractive glass jars. These soaks won't take the place of a water softener, so if you're accustomed to adding a softener, continue to do so. Add it before the soak material.

SALT SOAK

It's an amazing feeling to bathe in salt water. It not only relieves fatigue, but makes your whole body feel silky.

Start running warm water into the tub and then add 1½ cups ordinary table salt to the bath. Have the water nice and warm but not hot. Salt will cut down a little on the lathering properties of your soap, but who cares when you feel so fine?

OATMEAL SOAK

Good for easing a sunburned skin or one that's just dry and tired. It coats you with a velvety fragrance.

1 cup oatmeal (noninstant)

½ cup orrisroot (powdered)

Crush the oatmeal flakes a little so they'll release their minerals when you add them to water. Mix with the orrisroot, and place in the center of a piece of plain fabric, and tie into a ball. Take the ball into the bath, and after it has soaked awhile, rub it over your skin. The ball can be used over again, as many times as it seems to be doing its job.

Effervescent Soak

A mild bubbly soak.

> 5 ounces tartaric acid
> 5 ounces bicarbonate of soda
> 3 ounces cornstarch
> 6 drops oil of lavender, rosemary, or rose geranium

Crush and mix the first three ingredients in a bowl. Place in a glass jar and drop in the oil, then close the jar tightly and shake several times a day for 2 days to develop fragrance. To use, start hot water and drop about half a cup of the mixture into the tub as it fills.

Calming Soak

My mother always bathed us in baking soda water after we had a fever. I remember those occasions with the same warmth that I feel for milk toast—a treat we only had when we were feeling "poorly." Baking soda (from the kitchen) has a tranquilizing effect, and its alkaline action soothes all kinds of prickly miseries. It also removes perspiration odors.

Add about 1 cup to a tub of water.

To transform the above soda bath into a glamorous product, fill a pint glass jar almost to the top with baking soda. Leave just enough space at the top so the contents can be shaken effectively. Using an eyedropper, add one of the following essential oils, or a mixture of them. Allow the jar to stand at least a week in a place where it can be picked up and given a shake now and then.

For an oriental fragrance, add 2 droppers of essence of ylang-ylang.

For a bouncy fragrance, add 1 dropper oil of rosemary.
For a regal fragrance, add 1 dropper oil of lavender.

Bubbles

A few years ago I accidentally discovered a "down-home" substitute for an elegant bubble bath. Our water is exceedingly hard, so I'd been buying bath softeners. One day I added my household detergent instead. It was a sensational experience—frothy bubbles all the way to the top of the tub that lasted through a long bath.

There are detergents and detergents though, so choose a light-duty, nonalkaline brand—one that will not dry your skin. A bulletin from the U.S. Department of Agriculture in 1971 listed thirteen different name brands of light-duty detergents.

I made my first experiment with Trend, but this doesn't mean it's the best of the bunch. It is, however, clear in color and almost scentless, so it is easy to glamorize.

SCENTED BUBBLES I
An elegantly scented brew.
4 cups Trend
4 droppers tincture of ambergris
4 droppers tincture of musk
4 droppers tincture of civet
4 droppers oil of orange
1 dropper oil of clove
Red food coloring (I used 4 drops)
Fill a glass jar with the first 6 ingredients and gradually drop in the food coloring to the shade you want. Don't

stir too violently or you'll get the detergent all frothy. Let the mixture set for about 5 days to develop the scent.

One quart lasts a long time, for only ¼ cup fills the tub with bubbles. It can be packaged in containers like steak sauce or bitters bottles. An empty mouthwash bottle is nice, too.

SCENTED BUBBLES II

This needs no color. It has its own fragrance but changes with the addition of the following ingredients. It becomes spicy.

2 cups liquid Lux detergent
4 droppers oil of bergamot
4 droppers oil of lavender
2 droppers tincture of musk

Stir and let stand 5 days before using. Use ¼ cup to a tub of water.

Royal Bath Puddings

These puddings are a good way to add oil to the bath without having the tub (or you) feel greasy. They contain the yolk of an egg and create an almost sinfully rich bathing experience. An excellent gift, but they should be refrigerated. They will last 2 to 3 weeks. The color is golden, and I've purposely chosen delicate scents to complement the color.

VANILLA PUDDING

A fragrance like homemade Christmas pudding.

1 egg yolk
¼ cup safflower or sesame oil

9 drops oil of bergamot
6 drops oil of lavender
2 drops oil of verbena
9 drops tincture of ambergris
9 drops tincture of musk
2 cups water

Beat the egg yolk in a small bowl until frothy. Add the essential oils to the vegetable oil. Gradually add the combined oils to the egg yolk and continue to beat until they're well blended. Adding ¼ cup of water at a time, gradually add all the water, beating thoroughly with each addition. Store in the refrigerator. Shake before using. Use ¼ cup per bath.

ORANGE PUDDING

Smells like oranges that have been grown for the Emperor.

Follow the directions for Vanilla Pudding (above), but substitute 1 dropper oil of orange and 1 dropper essence of ylang-ylang for the essential oils.

SPICE PUDDING

Follow directions for Vanilla Pudding (above), but substitute 1 dropper oil of cinnamon and four drops oil of clove for the essential oils.

Bath Silks

I thought at first I'd call these mixtures "milks" because they look so much like those old-fashioned bottles of nonhomogenized milk—with the cream still intact. But everyone who tested them argued that they should be labeled "silks" because of the silky feeling they left on the skin.

The body should be patted dry rather than rubbed in order to have the fragrance hang on a little longer.

Let silks age 48 hours before you use them; this allows the combination of scents to become friendly. The gum arabic in the formulas acts to blend the oil and water so they won't separate in the tub.

LAVENDER SILK

An English garden scent—the early morning kind when dew is still on the leaves.

 2 tablespoons safflower or sesame oil
 2 droppers oil of lavender
 2 tablespoons gum arabic (powdered)
 1 cup water

Combine the oils. Make a smooth paste by placing the gum in a bowl and adding the oils, a few drops at a time. Be sure the paste is free of lumps. Begin to add water, a spoonful at a time. When you have enough volume, beat with an egg beater, continuing to add water until the whole cup is added. The solution will turn milky in color as you beat. Place in a glass botttle and store in the refrigerator. Use about ¼ cup per tub.

LAVENDER SILK WITH CINNAMON

A spicy fragrance that both men and women enjoy.

 ¼ cup safflower or sesame oil
 24 drops oil of lavender
 12 drops oil of cinnamon
 2 tablespoons gum arabic (powdered)
 2 cups water

Proceed as with Lavender Silk (above).

LAVENDER SILK WITH CLOVE

When plain old clove and lavender combine they create a scent that makes anyone's body feel cherished. It's one of my favorite scents.

Follow directions for Lavender Silk substituting 1 dropper oil of clove for the cinnamon.

Bath Perfumes

Nothing you can put into the tub makes you feel more pampered than bath oil. Even knowing you'll probably have to wash away the residual film of oil from the tub doesn't detract from the enjoyment.

GOLDEN LEMON OIL (Concentrated)

A spicy-lemon after-fragrance with a bright copper color.

> 2 tablespoons glycerine
> ¼ cup castor oil
> 2 droppers saffron coloring (see page 158)
> 1 dropper oil of lavender
> 1 dropper oil of rosemary
> 1 dropper verbena oil compound

Place all the ingredients in a glass jar and shake well. Put on a tight-fitting lid and allow to age 48 hours before use.

To use, soften the bath water first as you normally do, then use 1 or 2 tablespoons oil per bath. Some of the droplets float like miniature lily pads. Float them over to your body and massage them into dry spots. This leaves a fragrant sheen. Note: The color is optional—very pretty, but not necessary.

PINK PERFUMED OIL

A fresh scent of honey and orange juice.

¼ cup glycerine
1 cup water
2 droppers oil of rose geranium
2 droppers oil of orange
10 drops oil of patchouli
1 drop red food coloring

Place all the ingredients together in a glass jar and shake well. Glycerine mixes with water, but you will probably have to shake before using anyway.

PATCHOULI OIL

An aroma that floats in the air all day long and even seems to change from time to time. It's a favorite of my husband, and it does make him exceedingly attractive. If you color it (as in the recipe), it will have two layers of color—one a deep purple and the other violet. It looks beautiful in the jar.

¼ cup safflower or sesame oil
2 tablespoons glycerine
1 cup water
12 drops oil of patchouli
20 drops oil of rose geranium

Optional: 2 teaspoons color from alkanet root (see page 156 on color 3).

Mix the oils and water in a jar and shake well to blend. Shake again before using.

FOREST GREEN OIL (Concentrated)

A very powerful animal-like fragrance. It makes me think of headline stories about beautiful people.

¼ cup glycerine

3 drops green food coloring

10 drops oil of coriander

20 drops essence of ylang-ylang

10 drops tincture of musk

10 drops tincture of ambergris

5 drops tincture of civet

Mix all the ingredients in a glass jar. Shake well to blend. Cap tightly. Use sparingly.

LAVENDER CREAM

Excellent to use following a day in the sun or wind. It leaves a heavy film of fragrant oil all over the body.

2 tablespoons sal tartar (potassium carbonate)

2 tablespoons water

½ cup castor oil

2 droppers oil of lavender

Dissolve the sal tartar in the water and then add to the castor oil in a glass jar. Shake well to blend. Add the oil of lavender, shake again, then let stand 48 hours to age. It will have a creamy consistency. Use 1 or 2 tablespoons to a tub of water. Sal tartar can be purchased at most drugstores.

QUICKIE PERFUME OILS

After you've become familiar with the scents of the various essential oils, choose one of them or a combination of them to add to safflower oil. Measure out ¼ cup safflower and perfume it with 2 droppers oil of orange, for instance. You can try any combination you like. The safflower oil is not too heavy, and feels misty after the bath.

A CRYSTAL BATH PERFUME

A lovely turquoise color with a heady fragrance.

    2 cups table salt
    3 droppers oil of rhodium
    3 droppers tincture of musk
    10 drops yellow food coloring
    10 drops blue food coloring

Place the salt in a quart jar, then add the rest of the ingredients and shake until well blended. This is a variation of the expensive bath salts you see on drugstore shelves. It's fun to experiment with colors and with scents. It makes a beautiful gift and will keep indefinitely.

MID-SHOWER SCRUBBER

Actually, this mixture can be used in the shower, the tub, or during a sauna. It rubs away grime and murk from face, elbows, and knees. It's like giving your whole body a facial. To make 2 "scrubbers" use:

    1 cup oatmeal
    ½ cup almond meal
    ½ cup cornmeal

Place all three ingredients on a sheet of waxed paper and mix. Make 2 bags by cutting out 2 squares of fabric about 6 x 6 inches. Lay half the mixture on each square and tie into balls.

To use, wet the ball till it feels gummy and pliable. Rub briskly over the areas you want to polish and clean, then shower off. Repeat once again for a superior feeling. Almonds have been a favorite cosmetic ingredient for centuries.

Vinegars for the Bath

Household vinegar is pretty wonderful stuff. It can relieve a headache, act as a mouthwash, destroy odors, and clear the skin and scalp of old, flaky soap film.

The following vinegars are designed to perfume the bath while adding their own special properties to the bath water. They are sinfully easy to make, and if you gather your own plant material they will cost only the price of the vinegar. (I should point out that commercial cosmetic vinegars sell for five dollars a pint.)

GENERAL DIRECTIONS

Fill a one-pint glass jar with plant material to within 2 inches of the top. (This will be approximately 1 cup of material.) Bring 1 cup of a good-quality white vinegar just to the boiling point and pour it over the material in the jar. Put on a lid and let the materials blend for 2 weeks, keeping the bottle handy so you can shake it once or twice a day. At the end of 2 weeks, strain and pour into a decorative bottle. You can put a fresh sprig of the appropriate herb right in the bottle. It will remind you of the nature of the contents and look beautiful at the same time.

For use, add 1 cup to each tub of water. This will perfume the bath and make your body feel squeaky clean.

SWEET VIOLET VINEGAR

A very mild scent. You really have to work at it to

believe it's there, but it's worth the effort. Herbalists believe violets can cure headaches.

Use both the blossoms and leaves of scented violets.

Bath of Rose Vinegar

Rose petals are slightly astringent. The combination
of petals and vinegar is invigorating, especially if you
have access to roses with a spicy scent.

Float rose buds in the bottle after it's finished.

Lavender Vinegar

A delicate and sweet fragrance.

Use both the flowers and foliage. You can also bring up
the fragrance with powdered orrisroot. Use 1 tablespoon
to each pint of liquid. A sprig of lavender can be used as
a decorative item.

A Vinegar to Relieve Fatigue

Combine ½ cup wormwood (cut) with 3 bruised star
anise seeds.

Balmy Bath Vinegar

Balm has a natural lemony fragrance. The dried plants
can be used, but if you have access to fresh balm, be sure
to try this bath. Its aroma is cheerful and bouncy. One
cup of the dried material may be too heavy, for it is
stronger than the fresh balm.

Spicy Bath Vinegar

Combine ½ cup dried rosemary with ½ cup lavender.
Add a pinch of sage and 1 tablespoon bruised whole
cloves. Decorate with a sprig of rosemary.

MINT BATH VINEGAR

Since any of the mints give such a tang to foods, I like to think they can do the same for the skin. You can choose peppermint, spearmint, lemon, orange, or apple mint.

Vinegar can also be scented with essential oils. Start with 15 drops of oil to each pint of vinegar, and then adjust to suit yourself. Some I've made and enjoyed are:

Jasmine, 15 drops
Oil of orange and lemon, 8 drops each
Lavender, 12 drops, plus 3 drops oil of clove
Bergamot, 8 drops, plus 4 drops oil of rosemary
Essence of ylang-ylang, 20 drops, plus 5 drops tincture of ambergris

After-Bath Rubs

I have never understood why I liked walruses so much—or hippos and hedgehogs—until I read recently that these animals particularly enjoy physical contact. Other animals, like the horse and muskrat (and a lot of people) are noncontact species.

Physical contact is nice. I'm happy that it's become more acceptable among humans today. In addition to the normal, everyday kinds of physical contact that occur socially, you can do some really fine things for people if you learn how to do a massage properly. Massage stimulates circulation, increases suppleness, soothes the nerves, and just generally makes folks feel good. If you add perfumed oil or cream to the massaging process, it adds even more to the feeling of well-being.

Many bland vegetable oils (unadulterated by preservatives) can form the base of a body rub. Safflower, sesame, sweet almond, or coconut oil are the ones I use most often. Olive oil is excellent but has a heavy odor, which I object to. It is, however, a favorite of many people. Since many herbal oils have special healing or soothing properties, they can be combined with the vegetable oils to make special rubs. For example, eucalyptus oil, balm of gilead, and cajeput oil are said to be good for sprains, bruises, and aching muscles. Oil of clove is an old-fashioned remedy for pain. Thyme is used to relieve muscle pain and discomfort. These particular herbal oils are diluted for use because some of them are powerful enough to cause discomfort on the skin.

The back of this book has a list of herbal books for those who want to do extensive exploration in the subject. In the meantime, you can look over the recipes immediately following to give you an idea of possibilities.

Rub for Aching Feet

Combine 3 drops oil of clove with 3 tablespoons sesame oil. It makes feet smell like freshly baked cookies and takes away fatigue.

BACK RUB

For 1 rub, place 2 tablespoons coconut oil in a bowl and work in 10 drops essence of ylang-ylang. Coconut oil is nongreasy and semihard at room temperature. It will relieve surface tension.

RUB FOR ACHING LEGS OR SHOULDERS

Add 2 tablespoons oil of camphor to ½ cup sweet almond or sesame oil. This is very cooling, and excellent if your skin feels itchy or dry. It will keep for several months if tightly stoppered.

ACHING MUSCLES RUB

Cajeput oil has been used as a germicide in the Far East and in Australia. A good choice to relieve muscle pain.

Place 2 tablespoons almond or sesame oil in a saucer and add 3 to 6 drops cajeput oil. It's nice to warm it before you rub it on.

ANTI-DRY RUBBING CREAM

Soft, but not runny texture, with a fresh fragrance. This makes a beautiful gift. Recipe yields approximately 1 cup of cream.

 ¼ cup white wax chips
 1 ½ tablespoons lanolin
 6 tablespoons sweet almond oil
 2 tablespoons distilled water
 20 drops oil of lavender
 10 drops oil of rosemary
 20 drops oil of orange
 10 drops oil of bergamot
In a double boiler over hot water, melt the white wax,

along with the lanolin. Using a wire whisk, slowly add the almond oil. After the mixture is well blended, add the water, a few drops at a time, as you continue to whisk. Take from the fire and while still warm, but not hot, add the essential oils. Store in a closed glass container to preserve the fragrance.

MASSAGE BALL FOR ACHES AND PAINS

Very cooling and soothing. Made into the shape of a ball or oval, it's easy to store and easy to use.

> 1 single cake household paraffin (they come 4 to a box)
> 20 drops oil of wintergreen
> 20 drops oil of camphor

Melt the wax in a double boiler over hot water and drop in the oils, one at a time. Blend. Pour out into a slightly rounded dish, and when it's almost hard roll it into several round or oval balls that fit the hand comfortably. Use one to rub over whatever hurts. If you apply a little pressure, you can feel the spot grow warm. Store in a small box or wrap in foil between use.

Softeners

Some oils are used primarily for their softening qualities. The following skin softeners can be used any time, of course, but are especially effective after bathing. They make excellent massage oils, too. These oils will not need to be refrigerated, but they should be kept cool. Be sure to keep them tightly stoppered so their fragrance will last. For maximum results, keep the bottle in a dark place, or use an opaque bottle. To hold the fragrance together and to prevent the possible onslaught of rancidity, you can add 1 drop tincture of benzoin to every ounce of oil. Add it to the solution when you add the essential oil.

Skin Softener I

Peach kernel and castor oil both have softening properties. Combined with oil of lavender, the castor oil loses its oily scent.

> ¼ cup peach kernel oil
> 2 tablespoons castor oil
> 3 drops oil of lavender

Combine the ingredients in a small glass bottle. Keep tightly stoppered.

Skin Softener II

Gum benzoin has a vanilla-like aroma that becomes fragrantly woody when left on the skin.

> ½ cup safflower or sesame oil
> 2 tablespoons gum benzoin (powdered)

Place the oil in a pint bottle and add the gum benzoin. Shake well, then let stand for 2 weeks, shaking every day to develop fragrance.

Ylang-Ylang Softener

The blossoms of this tree give off a fragrance so heady that it makes people swoon. You may want to be very discreet, then, when you use this potion. I never felt like swooning, but it does have a mysteriously seductive effect when used as a massage oil.

> 6 tablespoons glycerine
> 3 tablespoons water
> 6 droppers essence of ylang-ylang
> 3 droppers oil of orange

Mix all the ingredients together in a glass jar and allow the flavors to blend for 24 hours. The softener disappears into the skin immediately, but the fragrance lingers for 2 or 3 hours.

HEAVY SOFTENER FOR CHAPPED BODY PARTS

Smells sweet and spicy. It needs to be thoroughly rubbed in, which can be a very nice experience. Lanolin is extracted from the wool of a sheep and has extraordinary softening qualities. (You may not like its sheepy odor.)

¼ cup lanolin
2 tablespoons sweet oil of almond
1 dropper oil of lavender
1 dropper oil of clove
8 drops tincture of musk
8 drops tincture of ambergris

Melt the lanolin over hot water, then add the other ingredients and mix well. Allow 48 hours for the fragrance to blend. Package in suitable containers and use sparingly.

CREAMY SOFTENER I

This cream goes on quickly. It disappears, in fact, almost immediately. Coconut oil provides a barrier against extremes of sun or wind, so this is good to use before going out into the elements or after coming back in.

¼ cup coconut oil
2 tablespoons oil of sweet almond
1 dropper tincture of ambergris

Blend the oils and ambergris in a bowl and transfer to a small jar with a screw cap. To give this an exciting animal-like scent, you can add 3 drops tincture of civet along with the ambergris. It changes the character of the mixture.

CREAMY SOFTENER II

Coconut oil leaves a faint glisten on the skin and melts at body temperature. It comes from the store in a semi-solid state. This scent combination is delicious, requiring 5 different oils. It creates a fresh orange blossom fragrance.

> ½ cup coconut oil
> 20 drops oil of lavender
> 20 drops tincture of musk
> 10 drops oil of rosemary
> 10 drops oil of orange
> 10 drops oil of bergamot

Melt the coconut oil over hot water, and while it is still warm add the essential oils. Stir to blend completely and pour into a small glass jar with a screw top.

CREAMY SOFTENER III

Elder flowers whiten the skin and contain wonderful medical properties. They are a favorite among herbalists, being used (among other things) to relieve the pain of burns or scalds.

Place ½ pound coconut oil into the top of a double boiler. When it melts, add 2 or 3 handfuls of elder flowers. (If you are picking your own, try to preserve the pollen intact.)

Keep the lid on and let the water just barely simmer for 2 hours.

Strain away the flowers by placing a soft cloth in the bowl of a large kitchen strainer and pouring the mixture through. Add 8 drops tincture of benzoin and pour into small glass jars.

elderberry

Note: Lard will make a good substitute for the coconut oil.

LIQUID SOFTENER I

Apricot kernel oil is believed to be an enemy of wrinkles, and it is widely used to smooth away stretch marks. The outrageously spicy fragrance of this softener lasts for several hours. Don't get it in your eyes. It is powerful.

½ cup apricot kernel oil.

5 drops oil of cinnamon

Combine in a jar and shake to blend.

LIQUID SOFTENER II

Glycerine is easy to obtain, and is one of the finest cures I know of for chapped, roughened skin. It has superior emollient qualities. Slick and heavy, it demands time to rub it into the skin, but it's worth the effort.

Buy a 4-ounce bottle of glycerine and scent it by dropping in 8 drops oil of lavender or 12 drops tincture of ambergris. Other scents can be used, of course.

GLYCERINE COOLER

This has so much zip that it almost sings. It's great for hot summer days, or for those dry-winter-house days. This recipe is for a small amount, but it can, of course, be increased.

 2 tablespoons glycerine
 2 tablespoons fresh lemon juice
 2 droppers oil of orange

Combine in a small bottle and shake. Keep in the refrigerator. Be lavish with this; it feels so good.

ROSE WATER SOFTENER

My grandmother introduced me to this combination. It has an old-fashioned fragrance.

Mix 1 part rose water and 1 part glycerine in a jar. Keep on hand to soften the skin after bathing.

SOFTENER FOR DRY FEET

This has a superior fragrance. It's heavy, but worth the time it takes to rub it in.

 2 tablespoons lanolin
 1 tablespoon sweet almond oil
 1 tablespoon glycerine
 1 dropper oil of rose geranium
 1 dropper oil of patchouli

Warm the lanolin over hot water, then add the almond oil and glycerine. Add the essential oils and store in a glass jar.

Powders

Powder is used to dust on after a bath or to take away hot, murky feelings any time. Because it absorbs excess moisture, it soothes when rubbed into wrinkles and crevices.

Miracle Powder

The best remedy I've ever found for diaper or heat rash is ordinary household cornstarch. I have never known it to fail to clear up even harsh instances of diaper rash. It works miracles on the rash that develops when children have to be hospitalized for long periods, too. I keep it in a shaker-top bottle and use it lavishly in the summer.

Scented Talcum

I don't know why it is, but most talcum powder either smells like an oversweetened baby nursery or like medicated foot powder. Since I don't like to smell like either

one of those, and since I object to the high cost of bath powder, I came up with an alternative. Most talcum powder, by the way, consists of at least 80 percent talc, a form of soapstone.

I shopped until I found the least heavily scented of the commercial talcum powders and then used this as a base for my own after-bath powder. If you want to try the system, buy the large economy size, take off the top, and pour the contents into a clean glass jar. For a pint-sized container, I add 4 to 6 droppers of my current favorite cologne. The mixture is then shaken several times a day for several days to distribute the fragrance and to keep the talcum from caking.

Essential oils can be added to talcum in the same way. You'll have to experiment to see what oils will blend with the original scent of talcum powder. I like to use 3 droppers oil of coriander to a pint of talcum. It gives it an orangelike fragrance that is nice for an after-shave powder, too.

A combination of 20 drops oil of lavender and 8 drops oil of clove gives a clear, spicy fragrance.

SCENTED BATH POWDER

Orrisroot has its own mild fragrance, and is used in the perfume industry to hold other fragrances together. It's used here to combine and hold the odors of the essential oils. This is a super-elegant both powder.

    8 ounces cornstarch
    2 ounces orrisroot (powdered)

Place the above ingredients in a glass jar and shake to mix. Package in suitable containers.

If you want a headier scent, add one of the following to the above mixture:

6 drops oil of clove (spicy)
12 drops oil of lemon (citrus)
10 drops tincture of ambergris plus
2 drops oil of rhodium (elegant)

Shake each day over a period of 5 days, then package in suitable containers.

Fresh Flower After-Bath Powder

This is fun to make because it utilizes fresh flowers. You need a shoebox, 1 pound of cornstarch and 2 ounces of orrisroot. Blend the cornstarch and powdered orrisroot. Orrisroot will grab and hold the fragrance of the flowers you will be adding. In the meantime, line a shoebox with foil. Pour in the starch mixture, then take a piece of cheesecloth a little larger than the box and lay it over the starch. This will keep the flowers from getting mixed into the powder.

Now comes the fun part. Gather bark, petals, leaves, or other fragrant materials. Shake away any moisture and lay the material right on top of the cheesecloth. Close up the box securely and every few days check to see that none of the plants are moldy. If they are, toss them out. Each time you have access to more petals, and so on, add them to the box. Keep doing this, stirring the mix occasionally until it smells heart-rendingly delicious.

Remove the plant material, and if the powder has picked up moisture let it dry before you package it. Put it up in small containers that can be closed tightly.

Some suggestions for scenting materials:

Clover blossoms
Lilac blossoms

Mock orange blossoms
Lily of the valley blossoms
Mayflower (trailing arbutus)
Lavender (stems and blossoms)
Wild parsnip seeds
Peony blossoms

PACKAGING BATH POWDERS

A beautiful container can be made for powders by using one of the round, one-pound boxes that contain oatmeal. I save the lid, then cut off all but the bottom 4 inches of the box. The box is then decorated by gluing on some gorgeous, old-fashioned paper. A big, fluffy powder puff fits the container perfectly, and then the lid goes on. A small, squatty pint-sized jar is nice, too, especially if you add color to the powder.

Scented Herbal Waters

These waters are designed for an after-the-bath perfume. They can be used lavishly because they're so light. And because they have an alcohol base, they will leave the skin feeling tingly and cooled. They make an excellent after-shave lotion, too, or a bouncy splash for a hot day.

This group of waters takes advantage of the fact that, when herbs are steeped in alcohol, their fragrance and other properties are incorporated into the liquid. After the steeping period, the plant material is strained away and only the fragrant liquid remains.

GENERAL DIRECTIONS

To prepare an herbal water, you will want pint-sized glass jars, plant material (see the list that follows; sources for dried herbs are listed at back of the book), alcohol, and some interesting bottles for packaging the finished product. The alcohol used in these recipes is 80- or 90-proof vodka. It has no odor of its own (or loses it very quickly), so it doesn't clash with the herbs.

The process goes like this: Take 1 handful of the plant you choose and crackle or bruise it until it begins to give up its fragrance. Place it in the jar—this will usually fill it about half full—then add the alcohol to within an inch or so of the top. Screw on the lid and let the mixture stand for 2 weeks, shaking it every time you think of it so the flavors will develop. At the end of 2 weeks, check to see how fragrant it is. You may want to continue the steeping, or even add more herbs. If it pleases you as it is, strain out the herbs and bottle it. If it seems too strong, dilute it with distilled water.

SUGGESTED LIST OF FRAGRANT PLANT MATERIALS

BLOSSOMS
    Lilac
    Lily of the valley
    Magnolia
    Oleander
    Orange blossoms
    Tuberose
    Acacia

Lavender
Pinks

ROOTS AND SEEDS
    Ambrette seeds
    Khuskhus roots
    Lovage roots
    Sandalwood chips
    Wild parsnip seeds
    Coriander seeds
    Aniseed

LEAVES
    Lavender
    Lemon verbena
    Hyssop
    Rosemary
    Thyme
    Lemon balm
    Orange mint
    Strawberry

If you want to make an herbal water with astringent qualities, follow the directions for the scented herbal waters above, but use one of the following herbs:

Sage (leaves)	Rose (petals)
Chamomile (blossoms)	Elder (blossoms)
Horsetail (leaves and stems)	

Fresh strawberries make a divine, faintly scented astringent water. Crush ½ pound ripe strawberries and pour into a pint jar. Add ½ cup of vodka and shake each day for 3 days. At the end of the third day strain the liquid through several layers of cloth. Bottle for storage and use to rinse the face or body after a bath. Keep in the refrigerator.

SCENTED WATERS WITH OILS

To perfume the skin and refresh it at the same time, you can use one of the following recipes. These waters are easy to make, and they take the place of toilet waters sold at exorbitant prices. Packaged in beautiful old bottles, they can make exciting gifts.

All recipes should age at least 2 weeks before you make a judgment about their fragrance. At the start they may seem too sharp or pungent. They keep well and (like wine) extra aging mellows them and smoothes out the scent. If, after aging, the fragrance is too heavy to suit you, try adding ¼ cup of vodka.

The recipes all call for 1 pint of vodka, but they can be cut in half by reducing all the ingredients proportionately.

Sunrise Waters
A fresh, clean smelling water.
    1 pint 80-proof vodka
    6 droppers oil of lavender
    6 droppers oil of bergamot
    1 dropper tincture of ambergris
Pour the vodka into a glass jar, leaving a bit of headroom for shaking. Add the oils and shake well, then let stand for 2 weeks to age.

Musky Waters
Sinfully fragrant. A good gift for friends and lovers.
    1 pint 80-proof vodka
    2 droppers oil of lavender

10 drops oil of clove
20 drops tincture of musk
Follow the instructions for Sunrise Waters (above).

GOLDEN WATERS
This is crispy and bright.
1 pint 80-proof vodka
4 droppers oil of bergamot
4 droppers oil of orange
4 droppers oil of lime
3 droppers oil of lemon
2 droppers oil of rosemary
Follow the instructions for Sunrise Waters (above).

SUMMER EVENING WATERS
This evokes an image of a soft, dark evening with a new moon and a singing chorus of crickets.
1 pint 80-proof vodka
6 droppers oil of lavender
4 droppers oil of rosemary
3 droppers oil of orange
3 droppers oil of lemon
3 droppers oil of bergamot
5 drops oil of clove
Follow the instructions for Sunrise Waters (above).

SWEET SUBSTITUTES

*B*EING SHORT OF nearly everything they needed to survive in a new land, our colonial ancestors cheerfully improvised the necessary tools and supplies from the materials they found around them in the countryside. They wove candlewicks out of milkweed down, carved brooms from branches, made medicines and cleaning compounds from plants, and burned weeds to make lights for their homes. The materials they worked with were in complete harmony with nature.

Unfortunately, in the "countryside" of today, medicinal shrubs, plants, and cattails have been subdued by asphalt, gravel, and concrete. And no one is permitted the challenge of improvising a candlewick, broom, or lamp. In fact, we've all been so oversupplied and overindulged that the act of improvising a something from a nothing has become a form of recreation. People today seem happy to discover they can still choose the raw materials from which to make accounterments for their daily lives. They've gone back to making cakes, cookies, casseroles, and even soap from scratch.

Starting from "scratch" is not hard to do. It's fun, it's a challenge, and surprisingly enough (for something that's fun) it's economical. Once you get into the swing of it, you may find you can reduce your household purchases to a few simple items like vinegar, salt, and ammonia. I think you'll find, as I did, that you can do away entirely with products caught inside aerosol spray cans. The good thing is, the earth won't be getting hurt. For all those simple things are biodegradable, and none of them have to be propelled into the atmosphere from an aerosol can.

Ammonia is a very old cleaning product. It's quite inexpensive, and is available in supermarkets every place. There are two kinds—the clear and the kind that has an extra ingredient to make a sudsy action. The sudsy ammonia is a milky color. Household ammonia gives off a nasty odor when it's first opened that makes it seem cruel, but it's actually gentler on hands than a lot of strong detergents and soaps. Its good marks come from the fact that it cuts grease. It also increases cleansing action by making water wetter.

Baking soda (sodium bicarbonate) absorbs odors, cuts oil and grease film, and cleans delicate surfaces without scratching them. It has many toilet uses, too, such as brushing teeth and relieving itchy skin rashes. A bonus is that baking soda doesn't pollute rivers and streams.

Borax used for household purposes can be purchased under that name in supermarkets. Borax used in cosmetics should be purchased from a pharmacy. I couldn't understand the difference between the two boraxes even by questioning "authorities." I can only assume that borax packaged for household use is not chemically as pure as that which comes from a pharmacy. At any rate, borax performs as a water softener, suds booster, and as a mild household antiseptic. It dissolves slowly in water, so I usually add it to a small amount of very hot water and stir to dissolve it before I add it to the rest of the ingredients.

Charcoal is Mr. and Mrs. Wonderful in the deodorizing department. It absorbs odors as though that was its precise and only purpose in life. Old sailing ships carried water in casks that were charred on the inside. Meats and vegetables were also stored in charcoal in order to preserve them from the obnoxious changes that would make them difficult or impossible to eat. If I understand it correctly, charcoal has the ability to absorb 90 times its own bulk in gases.

Vinegar has been a long-time favorite of folks who clean houses and folks who just live in them. It cuts greasy film, removes chemical deposits from pots and pans, and absorbs odors.

Substitutes for the Bathroom and Kitchen

Bathroom Enamel or Porcelain To remove stains or soap scum, add 1 cup ammonia to 1 quart water. Saturate a sponge and use to rub away stains.

Chrome Fixtures 1. Water spots disappear and fixtures shine without polishing if you wipe them with a solution of ¼ cup ammonia to 1 quart water.

2. Dampen a sponge with water and dip into a saucer of baking soda. Rub, then rinse and dry. Fixtures will sparkle.

Tile Walls Wash walls with a solution of 1 cup ammonia to 1 gallon water. Soap scum and water spots won't stand a chance.

Shower Curtains Use the same solution as above for tile walls. Lay out the curtain on a flat surface and sponge to remove mildew or rust discoloration.

Combs and Brushes 1. Soak in a solution of ½ cup ammonia to 1 quart water for 15 minutes. Rinse in hot water.

2. Soak in a solution of 3 tablespoons baking soda to a wash basin of warm water. Rinse in clear, hot water.

3. Soak for 15 minutes in a solution of ½ cup borax to a basin of hot water. Rinse in clear, hot water.

Kitchen Enamel and Porcelain 1. To clean enamel surfaces of cookware, china, refrigerators, stoves, and so on, scrub with a solution of ½ cup borax to 2 quarts warm water.

2. Rub Formica or other plastic surfaces with a dampened sponge that has been dipped into baking soda. Rinse with warm water.

Floors To remove built-up floor wax from tile and linoleum, add 2 cups ammonia to a bucket of warm water. Slosh the water on generously and allow it to lie there several minutes. Then rub vigorously. Do a small portion of the floor at a time. Rinse with clear water. Caution: Strong ammonia shouldn't be used on hardwood floors because it can remove the varnish.

Pots and Pans Borax has a nice, slow, unabrasive cleaning action. Sprinkle it on wet pots and pans and rub as though you were using cleanser. It won't scratch. Rinse and dry.

Refrigerator 1. Add ½ cup ammonia to 1 gallon water to clean refrigerator and freezer racks. Soak the racks a few minutes and then scrub and rinse. Odors will disappear.

2. Clean the interior walls of your refrigerator with a solution of 3 tablespoons baking soda to 1 quart water. Rinse and dry. This will remove odors along with stains.

Stove Burners Soak caked and blackened stove burners for 15 minutes in a solution of 1 part ammonia to 1 part water. Then scrub with a metal pot scrubber.

Burned Food Residue on Pans Make a paste using 3 tablespoons baking soda and just enough water to hold it together. Rub on the burned spots and let soak for 5 minutes, then rub with a sponge. Rinse and dry.

Oven Walls To remove hard crusty deposits on oven walls and boiler pans, set an open sauce dish of full-strength ammonia in the oven with a cloth "wick" hanging over the side of the dish. Close the oven door and leave overnight. In the morning wipe clean. Repeat the process for hard-core cases.

Cutting Boards Rub with a damp sponge dipped in baking soda, then rinse well with clear water. This will deodorize and clean.

Glass Coffee Pots 1. Wash the interior with a solution of 3 tablespoons baking soda to 1 quart warm water. Rinse with clear, warm water.

2. Half fill the pot with warm water. Add 2 tablespoons ammonia. Shake and wash, rinse well in clear water. This will remove film.

Glass Bottles and Vases Put a solution of 1 part vinegar to 1 part water inside hard-to-clean bottles. Shake until clean, then rinse with clear water.

Glassware Add vinegar to the rinse water when washing glassware. It will eliminate soap film.

Substitutes for Cleaning Automobiles and Outdoor Equipment

Seat Covers To clean vinyl or plastic seat covers, use a damp sponge dipped in baking soda. Wipe clean and rinse with warm, clear water.

Windshields 1. To clean windshields inside or out, wash with a damp sponge dipped in baking soda. Rinse well and rub dry.

2. Wash with a solution of ½ cup ammonia to 1 gallon water.

Tires, Chrome, and Radiator Grills Use a strong solution of ammonia—1 part to 2 parts water.

Battery and Terminals Scrub with a solution of 1 tablespoon baking soda to 1 quart water. "Paint" the solution on; rub well, then rinse. When dry, coat with petroleum jelly (Vaseline).

Fiber Glass Boats Use a wet sponge dipped in baking soda. Rinse with clean, clear water.

Bait Buckets Ugh! Three tablespoons baking soda to a bucket of water will render bait buckets socially acceptable. Scrub well and then rinse away the soda water.

Cooking Pots Scrub with a solution of 3 tablespoons baking soda to 1 quart water. Rinse.

Wrought-Iron Furniture Clean it of grease and other urban pollution with 1 quart water to which you've added 1 tablespoon baking soda. Rinse and dry well.

Wicker Furniture Wash with a solution of 2 tablespoons baking soda to 1 gallon warm water. Don't be afraid to wet wicker furniture. It likes it.

Substitutes for the Rest of the House

Painted Walls and Woodwork Add 1 cup ammonia, ½ cup vinegar, and ¼ cup baking soda to 1 gallon warm water. Wash with a soft cloth and rinse with clean, warm water.

Varnished Woodwork Varnished woodwork will respond to a cleansing solution made of tea. Save tea leaves (or bags from several days' tea) or use 4 fresh tea bags. Steep the tea in boiling water for 10 minutes. Cool and strain into ½ gallon warm water. The tea acts in the same way as a detergent. Wash the woodwork and then rinse with clear water.

Windows and Mirrors Add ½ cup ammonia to each quart of warm water. Wash the windows with a soft cloth, changing the water when it gets dirty. Dry with a clean soft cloth. If you are doing a large number of windows, put the solution into one of those manually operated spray bottles that are used to dampen clothes or spray plants.

Cleaners and Polishes for Furniture Natural polishes will be kind to your fine furniture no matter how many times a week you use them. They can be made up in fair-sized amounts and bottled for use.

1. A truly organic polish for beautiful wood can be made by simply rubbing the wood with the leaves of balm, a roadside plant. Its oil has a lemon fragrance. Mixed with equal parts of boiled linseed oil, it will leave a fine fragrance behind. Oil of balm is available from herbalists.

2. If you can find a source for kerosene today, and don't mind the oil-like after-smell, mix up a solution of 1 cup boiled linseed oil and 1 cup kerosene. It does not polish, but it clears away grime like it had never been there. Apply with a soft cloth. Store the cleaner in a glass jar; it will last a very long time.

3. A superior creamy polish can be made by grating 2½ ounces of beeswax into a tin can and setting the can

Bee balm

in a pot of warm water to melt. When melted, mix with ½ pint of turpentine. Don't put turpentine or wax directly on the fire!

In another pan, dissolve 1 ounce of castile soap along with 2 tablespoons powdered rosin in 2 cups of water. When dissolved, add to the can containing the turpentine mixture.

Pour into a glass jar for storage. This is a lovely polish. Rub on a small amount at a time and rub down with a soft, dry cloth.

4. A "slicker" for fine furniture can be made by pouring ⅔ cup cider vinegar into the blender and slowly adding ⅓ cup safflower or sweet almond oil until the two are blended. This is a super cleaner—not a wax. To use, pour onto a cloth and rub into the furniture. It will make wood look well loved.

Natural Household Deodorants

Aromatic Herbal Vinegars   Aromatic vinegars will soak up unwanted odors and cigarette smoke. They are easily made from household spices, herbs, and flowers, and can be set about the house in pretty bowls, where they will go to work dissipating odors. To make the aromatic vinegar, fill a 1-pint glass canning jar with fragrant material. (You can consult the list of fragrant materials, pages 17–20.) Heat 1 pint of white vinegar to the boiling point and pour it over the plant materials. Cover with a lid and let the mixture stand for 2 weeks, shaking it each day to keep reminding it that you care. Check it at the end of that time, and if you are satisfied with the scent, strain and pour into a decorative jar until you want to put it to use. You can enliven the vinegar with essential oils if you like, but I find that the odor from the essential oils doesn't hold up as long as that from plants. It can, of course, be refreshed occasionally simply by adding more oil. If you want to give a jar of the vinegar as a gift, put a sprig of something beautiful in it, like a sprig of nasturtium with its yellow flower or a sprig of mint or dill.

Household Vinegar and What It Can Do It can do a lot. To overcome especially powerful cooking odors, simmer vinegar on the stove. Add fragrance by adding cinnamon, cloves, anise, or some other strong spice.

When a jar has done its work as a pickle or mayonnaise or jelly container, and you want to use it to store something that smells different, you can get rid of the original odor by washing the jar thoroughly in hot water and then rinsing it with vinegar. If it's a very strong odor, let the vinegar set in the bottle overnight with its cap on. Vinegar is especially handy when working with essential oils used for some of the cosmetic recipes in this book. Utensils, thermometers, measuring spoons, and so forth can all be deodorized by soaking them in a vinegar rinse.

In the bread box, vinegar can be used to dampen a slice

of stale bread. Placed in the bread box overnight the bread will overcome that musty smell bread boxes seem so fond of. Repeat several times if you need to.

Doing dishes (by hand) can be a hateful chore after a fish dinner. You can cut down on both the odor and the oiliness of the fish if you add several tablespoonfuls of vinegar to the wash water. Soak the cooking pans before washing in a solution of 3 tablespoons baking soda for each quart of water.

Cooking and Other Unwanted Kitchen Odors When you are deep frying, add a sprig of rosemary to the fat. It will not completely overcome the cooking odor, but it helps a lot.

Cabbage doesn't smell very nice when it's cooking. Neither do broccoli, cauliflower, or turnips. You can throw a few red pepper pods into the cooking pot to subdue the odors. Savory leaves from the spice cabinet will do the same trick. Or, if you have some charcoal that's been untreated by additives, throw a chunk of this into the pot. Don't use charcoal that's been treated to ignite quickly. Untreated charcoal can be ordered from botanical supply houses and some drugstores. Charcoal has many household uses, and is inexpensive.

You can cut down on the stale odors emanating from a drain by pouring about half a cup of ammonia down the drain once a week. This will also help to keep it free flowing. One cup of baking soda will do the job, too. Let it set for 5 minutes, then flush through with hot water.

Pour ½ cup ammonia into the garbage disposal once a week to keep it fresh.

If the odor of the garbage pail has gotten out of hand (or before it does), wash the container with a solution of hot water, borax, and soapy water. Let it dry thoroughly and then sprinkle fresh, dry borax into the bottom before putting a liner in it. Each time you change the liner, put fresh borax in the bottom. This will help keep an outdoor container fresh and sweet, too.

Place a saucer of ammonia in the refrigerator while you're defrosting it. It will absorb stale odors and leave a fresh one behind.

Keep a box of baking soda (open) on the refrigerator shelf. It works away silently and leaves no odor of its own. Replace it about every 2 months, then pour it down the kitchen drain. It will help flush unpleasant odors from those quarters, too.

To freshen thermos bottles, fill about halfway to the top with water, add ¼ cup ammonia, shake several times, and then wash well. Rinse with clear, warm water.

When the can opener is washed, rub fresh lemon over its cutting edge to remove persistent unwanted odors.

Good-Time Scents for the Kitchen If you're going to be in the kitchen for a long time and want to treat your nose to some good-smelling items, get out the egg poacher and fill the cups with water. (A saucepan will do, too.) Look around the spice cabinet and choose spices to drop into the cups to simmer as you work. Ginger, cinnamon, aniseed, fennel seed, caraway, and cloves are all nice. Use

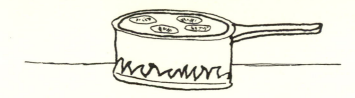

them alone, together, or mixed with other nonspice items. Sage is nice, and rosemary is delicious.

In a fit of energy one time I made up a special jar of scented material for these "good-time" scents. I used a base of sandalwood chips mixed with broken cinnamon sticks. The proportions weren't crucial. I threw in some patchouli leaves and some powdered frankincense and myrrh. Now I keep a container of these herbs handy all the time and use them whenever I want the kitchen to smell heavenly. Naturally, the scent is good for the whole house.

Scents and De-Scenters for the Rest of the House

Musty Smells 1. Musty smells that develop from keeping a room closed up for long periods of time can be alleviated if, before you close the doors, you place open containers of charcoal around the room.

2. Closed-up linen closets and dresser drawers will appreciate the fragrance of lavender flowers, lemon verbena, or lemon geranium leaves. Placed in the closed area, they will even keep it from taking on a musty smell.

3. Place bowls of ammonia in a room that's been closed up. Leave them overnight and they will take away odors. Repeat if necessary.

4. Clothes closets can be cheered up by soaking a few cotton balls in oil of patchouli. Leave them there for several days with the door closed. Your clothes will smell like those wonderful imported Indian shirts and skirts.

5. People at the Indiana Botanic Gardens say that a

mixture of 4 teaspoons baking soda in a quart of water will clear a room of unpleasant odors. They suggest putting this mixture into one of those hand-operated spray bottles. The mixture is to be sprayed around the room in a fine mist.

Ashtrays Wash in a solution of warm, soapy water with a small amount of ammonia. A car ashtray can be partially filled with baking soda. The soda will snuff out the butts and absorb odors.

Flower Vases It doesn't seem appropriate that something that goes into a vase smelling so wonderful can cause such an unpleasant smell later on. But we all know it does. For really hard-core, desperate cases, soak the vase overnight in a basin containing ¼ cup ammonia. Wash and rinse it in the morning and it will be all better.

Paint Odors Even paints advertised as nonsmelly have an odor that's not too pleasant. Keep a bowl or two of vinegar around to absorb these odors while you're painting a room. A bowl of vanilla extract works too, but is more expensive.

Accidents Every now and then, as most parents know, a child will have a nighttime accident and wet the bed. Sheets and blankets can be removed immediately and washed. But the mattress is another matter. Treat the mattress by sprinkling a small amount of water over it and rubbing borax into the damp area. Let the borax dry and then vacuum it away.

Kitty Litter Pans Put a cup of baking soda in the bottom of the pan before adding fresh litter.

Diaper Pails A gallon of water with ½ cup borax added to it is a good soak for diapers after they've been rinsed and while they're waiting to be washed. This will not only cut down on odors but will help condition them for washing.

Toilet Bowl Once a week pour 1 cup ammonia into the toilet bowl and leave it overnight with the lid down. The next day scrub with a brush to remove stains and odors.

Deodorants for People

Everybody needs to perspire. It's one way the body works to maintain an even temperature. But from listening to television commercials it would seem that perspiring is a social evil second only to the kicking of small dogs. I think it would be terrible if everyone smelled exactly the same—that is, had no particular scent of their own. Some scientists today believe that people do have their own particular scent, in the same way that animals do. One of them even suggests that it would be a good way for people to select a mate. Or, if not that, that they should at least check out a prospective mate's odor before they make a final decision. I'm not talking here about bad smells, but about the natural, everyday ones that indicate our humanness.

The following suggestions for substitutes for spray (and other) deodorants aren't going to work for everyone simply because we don't all have the same body chemistry. But there's not much lost by trying the different ones out to see how they work for you.

Witch hazel (available at drugstores) has a nice fresh woody odor and can be used for an underarm deodorant. It's very inexpensive. Witch hazel is a small shrub that grows wild and free. So even the thought of it is nice. Vinegar can also be used. The vinegar odor will disappear in just a few minutes. Neither one of these will stop wetness, and I would guess they'd need to be used every 4 hours if they're to be completely effective against odor. You can add herbs to the vinegar if you want to glamorize it. Rosemary has healing properties and a fresh smell. Myrrh, orrisroot, lavender, and chamomile are all mild and fresh.

Bugs and Baddies

I know that some bugs do good work, but I have a hard time being pleased about that fact. I wouldn't mind seeing legislation barring all gnats, mosquitoes, and flies from the earth. Mosquitoes and black flies have actually driven horses insane, and at times I have believed they were going to do the same for me. I think I could get along without them entirely, and to that end I've come up with a fairly long list of botanical items that are supposed to be helpful against those hateful creatures. Determined to find one that works for me, I'm still experimenting, so I can't give any of them an out-and-out unqualified recommendation. Some of them work for a while and then mysteriously quit being effective. If any of my readers discovers a repellant that really works without smelling ferocious, I will be here, ready to receive all good reports.

Okay, here's a list of possibilities:

GNATS

One reference source said mint repelled mosquitoes and gnats and that thyme attracted them. Another source said thyme could be used to repel them. See! Nobody can win in the battle against these fellows.

MOSQUITOES

Here is a quotation from the *1965 Herbalist Almanac* that shows how desperate people are to believe anything when it comes to this pest:

"Open windows wide and stretch across each one and across the door-opening, a piece of red ribbon 2 inches wide. It is said that a mosquito will never pass a red ribbon."

To be more practical, there are many essential oils that can be used. They can be mixed half and half with castor oil, for castor oil in itself will repel insects. Lavender, cloves, and sassafras are quite pleasant. Clove is strong, so be careful to keep it away from the eyes. Oil of pennyroyal is an all-time favorite of woodsmen. It can be used without dilution if the occasion demands it. It can also be mixed with Vaseline if a creamy consistency is desired. Oil of citronella is supereffective, but I find the odor difficult to live with. Oil of verbena or lemongrass are not terribly effective, but they do a fair job and the odor is very nice. To increase their powers, mix them with pennyroyal. Strong tea made of leaves and flowers of chamomile is sweetly fragrant and mildly effective.

FLIES

What can you say? I guess we need them, but I don't want to think about the reasons why. Here's what the *1965 Herbalist Almanac* has to say about flies:

"A few drops of Sassafras oil scattered about the house will keep flies away as if by magic.

"Bunches of red clover blossoms are said to be so offensive to flies as to bar them out of rooms containing them.

"Dip a bunch of plantain or fleawort in milk and hang it up in a room."

AFTER THE BIG BITE

Several herbs have properties that can take away the pain and sting of insect bites.

Vinegar will relieve the sting of a mosquito bite. Swab it on with a paper towel.

A tea made of rosemary is good for all kinds of bites and stings. So is hyssop. Make up a batch by steeping a handful of the herbs in a pint of water. Bring the mixture to a boil and then remove from the heat. Steep for 10 minutes. When it cools, keep it in the refrigerator.

Oil of sassafras cools stings and keeps the swelling down.

A dab of moistened baking soda on all kinds of bites helps relieve the insult and the pain.

MOTHS

Moths aren't the same problem today as they must have been during the last century. Old housekeeping books carried almost as many recipes for making moth repellants as they did for making cakes and pies. That could mean either that none of the recipes worked or that there were far too many moths per person to cope with. Moths eat holes in woolen clothing, and if they're left alone they can do an awfully good job of it. They also eat, or rather their larvae eat, mohair, natural bristle brushes, fur, and feathers.

Cedar and sandalwood are very effective against these beasts, and they smell very nice. Camphorwood, tobacco leaves, or whole cloves are useful, too. All these can be used several ways. Cotton balls can be scattered in closets and kept saturated with the oils of the botanicals. If clothing is to be stored over the summer by placing it in boxes or trunks, pieces of the wood, wrapped loosely in cheesecloth, can be placed in the container right along with the clothing. A more aesthetic way of handling the moth problem is to make cloth envelopes (like sachet bags) to hang throughout the closets. A mixture of aromatic herbs from the following list can be used:

Sandalwood
Camphorwood
Southernwood
Wormwood
Gray Santolina
Tansy

Mix them with such spices as whole cloves, peppercorns, thyme, mint, cinnamon, and cassia.

To lay in with linens or clothing, use sweet woodruff, lavender, or patchouli.

Substitutes for Cosmetics and Health Products

TOOTH CLEANERS

Tooth cleaners on the market contain such various items as soap, chalk, camphor, cuttlefish bone, and even marble dust. The more I think about those ingredients, the more pleased I am at my own simple dentrifice of baking soda and salt. I don't want to get you in trouble with your dentist, so if you want to switch from the dentrifice you've been using to one of the suggestions that follow, maybe you should check with him to see if he'll give his approval. Mine tells me I can use baking soda and/or salt at my discretion.

1. Kitchen baking soda is an extremely effective tooth powder that refreshes and cleans and does no abrading of the teeth. You can use it, as is, by pouring about half a spoonful into the palm of your hand and dipping your moistened toothbrush into it.

Or baking soda can be enriched by adding powdered herbs to it. I like to make up just half a pound at a time to keep it fresh and uncaked. To ½ pound baking soda, add 1 tablespoon powdered orrisroot. This will give the soda a violet scent. Orrisroot is very mild. Mothers used to give their babies orrisroots to chew on when they were teething.

To ½ pound baking soda, add 1 ⅔ tablespoons powdered gum myrrh. Gum myrrh will leave a refreshing taste in the mouth. Our forefathers used myrrh to heal ulcerated gums.

To ½ pound baking soda, add 1 ounce Peruvian bark. Peruvian bark has slight astringent properties. It's bitter (this is the stuff from which quinine is extracted), so you'll probably want to scent it. Drop 6 drops oil of clove (which also has germicidal properties) onto a small chunk of absorbent toweling or blotting paper. Put the paper into a closed container with the baking soda and give it 3 or 4 days to develop the scent. Don't drop the clove oil directly onto the soda, because it is powerful stuff and you wouldn't want a concentration of it to surprise you.

Other oils can be added, too, that are more fun than cloves—like oil of lemon or lime. Strawberry is nice, and cinnamon, too.

2. Herbs can be used alone as tooth cleaners. Mix the herbs; store in convenient, dry containers and use by putting a pinch of them in your hand and dipping into it.

Mix 2 ounces powdered gum myrrh with 2 ounces powdered orrisroot and get the good effects of both of these herbals. Keep dry.

Mix 2 ounces powdered goldenseal with 2 ounces powdered gum myrrh. Goldenseal has antiseptic properties. The Cherokee Indians used it as a mouthwash.

3. Powdered charcoal is an excellent dentrifice because it can clean, whiten, and deodorize simultaneously. Ordinary charcoal shouldn't be used, however; it may have additives, starters, or who knows what in it. You wouldn't want to accidentally ignite your mouth. Buy vegetable charcoal from health food stores or from herbalists. I only use charcoal once a week, but don't ask why. I guess I still associate it with fire and woodsmoke. Woodsmoke is not bad, but somehow it feels alien in my mouth. It sure does a nice whitening job, though.

4. Fresh strawberries can be rubbed on the teeth to whiten them. I can't do this though, even though their acid content can remove stains. When I get that close to a strawberry I have to eat it.

5. I don't know how far you're willing to go for a nice fresh mouth and white teeth, but you can make a super tooth cleaner from burned toast. People claim it really works. Scrape off the charred part into your palm and use it like any tooth powder.

6. One teaspoon vinegar in half a glass of water will refresh the teeth and gums and whiten them somewhat.

RECIPES FOR A FRESH MOUTH

MOUTHWASH I

Mix up equal amounts of salt and baking soda. Used as a mouthwash it will not only sweeten the breath but will help to keep gums firm. Use 1 teaspoon in a glass of water.

MOUTHWASH II

Make a tincture by adding 2 ounces powdered gum myrrh to 1 cup 80-proof vodka. Let it stand for 2 weeks, shaking it each day, then strain through several layers of fine cloth. Bottle for use and keep in the bathroom. When ready to use, pour out a teaspoon into a small glass of water and use as a mouthwash.

MOUTHWASH III

Place 1 pint of 80-proof vodka into a glass canning jar and add 2 tablespoons each powdered thyme, powdered sage, and powdered cloves. Put on the lid and allow the mixture to age for 2 weeks, shaking it each day. Strain through several layers of cloth and bottle for use. Use 1 teaspoon in a glass of water for a mouthwash.

BREATH-SWEETENING CHEWS

Following are some botanicals you can chew to make your breath instantaneously sweet:

> Angelica root
> Apples
> Cardamom seed (especially effective for alcohol
> breath)

Calamus root
Whole cloves
Nutmeg
Mace
Parsley (great against the smell of onions)
Star anise

To make medicine taking easier, bite into a fresh orange or lemon peel first. The aromatic oils will hide the taste. Be quick though—the effect only lasts a second or so.

SIMPLE SUN RECIPES

People keep warning other people about the effects of too much sun. I don't think anyone listens, though, for folks keep right on getting sunburn. Warnings will never be dire enough to keep people out of the sun entirely, for it's too nice a place to be. Everybody should use good sense about it, but, since they seldom do, here are some recipes to help ease the pain.

Apple cider vinegar, patted on, will relieve some of the agony of a fresh burn. Vinegar can even relieve the pain of extreme burns.

Cocoa butter can be used just as it comes from the drugstore to keep skin moist while sunning and to replace some of the moisture afterwards. It is semihard, but melts immediately on contact with the skin. In fact, it melts so easily that it can be a problem sometimes. Keep your eye on it and don't let it get too hot or it will spoil something. I like to add almond oil and scent to cocoa butter for a nice-smelling goo. I put equal parts of cocoa butter and almond oil in a pan over hot water, and when they're melted I add 1 dropper oil of lemon and 1 dropper oil of lime. I then pour it into an empty cold cream container. Both of these are excellent emollients, and the almond oil will help speed the tanning process.

Olive oil is another excellent emollient. Use it after exposure to the sun. It can be mixed with an equal amount of glycerine, and the cooling properties of oil of camphor or oil of eucalyptus added. Use 1 dropper of camphor or eucalyptus oil to each ounce of the emollient oil.

Witch hazel, poured into the palm and rubbed gently over a burning skin, will relieve some of the discomfort.

Crumble a cake of moist yeast into half a cup of vinegar and mash till both are united. Apply to sunburn for a cooling sensation.

When (or if) all else fails, a bath in a tub of warmish water, to which 1 cup of baking soda has been added, feels wonderful.

SCALP INVIGORATORS AND SHAMPOOS

INVIGORATOR I

You can encourage your scalp to create more luxuriant hair if you brush a rinse made of rosemary leaves into it once a week. Thyme will work also. Both of them have antiseptic properties.

Make a rinse by steeping a handful of rosemary or thyme in 1 pint of water. Bring the water to a boil; add the herb and let it steep until cool. Strain, then dip a brush into the mixture and brush until your hair is saturated. This rinse smells clean and green. If you can leave it on all night, it will have a better chance to work before you shampoo it away.

INVIGORATOR II

To stimulate your scalp and even get rid of dandruff or flakiness, make a paste of 1 cup salt and 5 tablespoons water. Rub this into your scalp with gusto and enterprise. Rest for 5 to 10 minutes, then brush the paste through the hair. Follow by a shampoo.

DRY SHAMPOO I

Make a dry shampoo for brushing through the hair when you don't have the time to wet-wash. It will leave the hair surprisingly glossy.

Take 1 cup of wheat bran cereal and reduce it to a coarse powder. Add and blend 1 ounce of powdered orrisroot. Sprinkle on your head like rain and brush through the hair several times.

DRY SHAMPOO II

Cornstarch will serve the same purpose as bran (above). Use 1 cup and add 1 tablespoon powdered orrisroot.

DRY SHAMPOO III

Mix 1 ounce powdered orrisroot with ½ pound salt. Rub into your scalp, brush through, and then brush out. Or you can leave it on and brush it out in the morning. If you add oil of violets to the mixture, your hair will smell wonderful.

LIQUID SHAMPOO

Easy to make, this shampoo also makes a good, mild body soap. I store it in a discarded plastic bottle with a pour cap.

Shave up 1 bar of castille soap and place in top of double boiler along with 3 cups distilled water. Heat slowly and stir until dissolved. Add 2 teaspoons potassium carbonate and 2 teaspoons borax, stirring to dissolve and blend. Remove from heat and add 6 droppers oil of lavender. Pour into quart container and add enough distilled water to make 32 ounces. Let it stand a week before using, to incorporate fragrance. Shake before using.

To use, wet the hair and pour about a tablespoon of the soap into the palm. Rub into the scalp; it's a delicious feeling. Oil of strawberry or oil of rosemary make good scents too.

HAIR RINSES

The following rinses will remove leftover soap film from the hair and condition the scalp naturally.

The simplest rinse is made by adding ½ cup cider vinegar to a quart of warm water and pouring it through the hair as a final rinse. It doesn't need to be rinsed away. The acetic odor will disappear in just a few moments.

Elder Flower Hair Rinse

The elder plant is highly regarded by herbalists. Flowers are used in a tea to unjangle nerves, and the leaves of the plants are made into an ointment to heal burns. You can make a hair rinse of the flowers to clear away all traces of soapy film and impart a healthy glow to the hair. The flowers can be ordered from herbalists. Or, if you want to look for it in the countryside, where it grows freely, its scientific name is *Sambucus canadensis*. It blossoms in May and June. The flowers can be gathered and dried for later use.

To make up 1 quart of the rinse, place ½ cup elder flowers into a quart glass jar. Fill the jar to the top with pure white vinegar and set it aside for at least a month, leaving it out in sight so you will be inspired to shake it at least once a day. After a month, strain out the flowers and bottle. To use, add ½ cup of the elder vinegar to your final hair rinse. Don't wash it away afterwards; the vinegar smell will dissipate rapidly.

LAVENDER HAIR RINSE

Flowers of lavender will give you a sweet-smelling rinse. Steep 2 handfuls of the flowers in pure white vinegar and follow directions (above) for Elder Flower Hair Rinse. Lavender flowers can be ordered from an herbalist.

OTHER HERBAL AND WILDFLOWER RINSES

Rinses can be made for the hair from many herbs and wildflowers. To make up a base material for herbal rinses, collect the dry material during the summer months and store it, following directions in the section on gathering and storing (pages 145–150). When dry materials are packaged with care, they will keep their special properties for a year. Any of the following plants can be used alone, or in combination with others.

Bee balm (it smells like ambergris)
Birch leaves
Comfrey (a natural disinfectant)
Clover blossoms
Fennel
Horsetail (a wild grass)
Lavender flowers
Lime flowers (linden)

comfrey

Marigold flowers
Rosemary (the whole plant can be used)
Speedwell (leaves and flowers)
Squirrel corn
Yarrow

When ready to make up a rinse, put ¼ cup of the dry mixture into 1 quart soft water. Bring to a boil and let it boil 2 minutes, then remove from the fire and let the brew steep for 20 minutes. Strain and use as a final rinse.

TREATMENTS FOR HANDS

Softener I

One or two drops of glycerine will soften the roughest, toughest cases of chapped hands. You wouldn't want to use it all the time, for it takes patience to rub it in. But it works even if hands are bleeding.

If you add an equal amount of lemon juice to glycerine, it will soften and whiten hands at the same time. And it is easier to rub in than pure glycerine.

If you prefer a creamy softener, work 1 ounce of glycerine into 1 tablespoon lard. It sounds terrible, but it's effective. Add 2 drops of an essential oil if you want to perfume it.

HAND SOFTENER II

This makes a creamy white softener. Coconut and almond oil are excellent emollients.

    1 ounce white wax chips (beeswax)
    ¼ cup coconut oil
    ½ cup sweet almond oil
    6 tablespoons glycerine
    6 droppers oil of lemon verbena

Heat the wax and coconut and almond oils together in a double boiler over hot water until the wax has melted and is blended with the oils. Gradually add the glycerine and stir until blended. Add the oil of lemon verbena for fragrance, then pour into a small jar and allow to cool. Keep covered.

HAND SOFTENER III

A softener with a natural, sweet fragrance.

    ¼ cup lard
    ¼ cup balsam of Peru

Melt together in the top of double boiler over hot water. The balsam has a persistent fragrance, so you may want to melt the two in a clean tin can over water rather than in a kitchen pot. When blended, pour into a small glass jar and keep tightly closed.

Hand Softener with Protein

    1 egg yolk

    ¼ cup glycerine

    2 droppers tincture of musk

Place the yolk in a small bowl. Add the glycerine and work into a smooth liquid, then scent with the tincture of musk. Place in a small glass jar and keep in the refrigerator. It smells heavenly.

A Soak for Chapped Hands

Red, chapped hands respond gratefully to a soak made of ¼ cup salt in a basin of warm water. Drop your hurting hands in the water and let them rest there for 10 minutes. Rinse and dry.

Hand Rubs

    1. After taking the hands out of hot, soapy water, rinse them in clear water and then, while they're still damp, take a pinch of cornstarch and rub it in. It will absorb all the wetness and make your hands feel silky.

    2. Oatmeal performs the same magic.

    3. If you want to remove ground-in dirt without resorting to harsh super cleaners, lather up with your regular soap and then put a pinch of oatmeal into the palm of your hands. Rub it in with the lather. It will not only cleanse, but will leave your hands feeling soft.

COSMETICS FOR YOUR LIPS

Lip Ice I

In a little pan over hot water, melt 1 tablespoon beeswax chips and 1 tablespoon coconut oil. Remove from the heat and add 1 dropper oil of rosemary. While still warm, pour into a small container. The rosemary has extraordinary healing properties.

This preparation can be used as a substitute for any of the lip ices that come in tubes and cost close to a dollar. I only make a small amount at a time, for it goes a long way.

Lip Ice II

Melt 1 tablespoon beeswax over hot water and combine with 1 tablespoon sweet almond oil. Add your scent while still warm. I like oil of lemon, and use 2 droppers for this amount of ice. You can add any of the fruit oils for fun. Try strawberry, orange, or grape, for example. They won't help heal chapped lips, but the almond oil does that job and it's fun to have strawberry lips. Or orange. Or grape.

Refresh-and-Dry Papers

You can make up your own disposable wash-and-dry papers and gear them to your own special needs. I'm not sure whether you can save money by doing these, for I haven't found an inexpensive source yet for the filter papers I use as a base. I buy 9-inch-square coffee filter papers. They are perfect for this use—soft, yet extremely durable and almost impossible to tear.

Depending on their proposed usage, I pour out the liquid into a flat baking dish, and one by one dip the filter papers into the solution. They are then packaged in foil (or in thin plastic wrap) in trip-sized packages.

When I want to make up a large number of papers at

a time, I package them by using one of those handy appliances that package and seal meals for the freezer. They are sold under a variety of trade names, but what they amount to is a sealing iron, plus a supply of strong, boilable plastic bags. Papers I've enclosed in these bags have stayed fragrant and moist for three months. I wouldn't want to suggest that you go buy one of those appliances just so you can make wash-and-dry papers. But if you already have one, you will want to take advantage of it for this purpose.

Here are some ways to use "papers":

1. A refreshing skin wash that smells wonderful and removes the grime of travel:

Equal parts rose water, lemon juice, and 80-proof vodka. Rose water is available from the druggist.

2. A wash to relieve itchiness or dryness:

Add 2 tablespoons glycerine to 1 cup less 2 tablespoons distilled water or rose water. Perfume with 2 teaspoons cologne or with one of the scents in the scent section (pages 119–121). This will moisturize and soften, too.

3. A wash that cleans and acts as a mild astringent; it smells clean:

   1 pint 80-proof vodka
   4 teaspoons orrisroot (powdered)
   2 droppers oil of rose geranium

Make this one up ahead of time. Put the first two ingredients into a glass jar and shake every day for 2 weeks. Strain, then add the oil of rose geranium.

4. Witch hazel (from the drugstore) is an excellent skin cleanser; it is also helpful in removing the sting of insect bites, burn of sunburn, as an after-shave lotion, and as a deodorant.

5. For a soapy cleaning-up job for children's hands and

faces, impregnate papers with the liquid soap on page 136–137.

6. Add 8 drops tincture of benzoin to 1 cup rose water for a superior, sweet-smelling facial cleanser.

7. Pour a bottle of baby oil into saucer and impregnate papers to use as a skin cleanser. Leave a second application on the face as a protection against sun and windburn.

8. A lovely herbal wash:

> 1 cup lavender flowers
> ¼ cup cloves (bruised)
> ¼ cup orrisroot (powdered)
> 1 cup 80-proof vodka
> ¼ cup glycerine
> Distilled water

Place all the ingredients except the glycerine and distilled water together in a glass jar and let set for 2 weeks, shaking each day. Strain through cloth to remove the plant material, then add the glycerine and enough distilled water to make 1 pint of liquid.

Sachets and Colognes

The manufacturing of perfume is an exotically complicated process, and many of the well-known brands are the result of years of splendidly guarded research. The high price of such scents indicates their luxury status. I have no intention of disparaging commercially manufactured perfumes. Some of them have made me extremely happy. But if what we perfume wearers want is to make ourselves and the atmosphere around us smell heavenly, then we can do that in a variety of ways, some of them as simple as wearing a gardenia in our hair.

SACHET OILS

A very simple way of making perfume is to blend an essential oil (the scented volatile oil of a plant) with a base of sweet almond oil. This combination will give you a skin sachet to wear on the inside of the arm, on the temples, or wherever you like to wear perfume. Almond oil is not only scentless in itself but is an excellent skin conditioner.

When working with essential oils, you will want to keep in mind that some of these oils are uninteresting by themselves but make beautiful music when they're blended with others. They also smell different on the skin than they do in the container. Experimenting with different blends is an exciting process that doesn't require a great outlay of cash.

To make the sachet oils, you will need several eye-droppers and some tiny bottles or jars that can be tightly stoppered. Both light and air attack the fragrance of the oils. Craft stores sell handsome slender glass vials with corks to fit that are about 3 inches high and an inch in diameter. They look like the ones used by physicians preparing life-saving serums. They cost only a few cents, are excellent for experimenting with scents, and are easy to wash and reuse. For permanent storage of scented oils, though, you would have to keep these bottles in a dark place or cover them with some beautiful paper.

Essential oils can be ordered from most firms that sell herbs. Some health food stores carry them, and drugstores carry a few of the more common ones. The terms "volatile oil" and "essential oil" are used interchangeably.

Note: An "extract" is not an essential oil, though it may appear on the same shelf with essential oils.

After blending the fragrant oils, let the mixtures stand two weeks before making a decision about them. Aging will change the blend.

Following are just a few scent combinations. There are at least eighty essential oils from which to choose, so the variety is endless.

SACHET OIL I

To a base of ¼ cup sweet almond oil, add 10 drops tincture of ambergris and 1 dropper tincture of musk.

SACHET OIL II

To a base of ¼ cup sweet almond oil, add 1 dropper oil of lavender and 1 dropper oil of clove.

SACHET OIL III

To a base of ¼ cup sweet almond oil, add 1 dropper tincture of ambergris and 1 dropper oil of rhodium.

CREAM SACHETS

Cream sachets are very subtle. I like them because they don't come on with a big attention-getting roar. There's an elegant kind of underplayed classiness to them. Be generous when you rub them on—they won't embarrass you. The recipes here make small amounts—about 1 cupful. Even this amount can be divided into two parts and scented with two different scents. Keep them in tightly stoppered glass containers. My favorite container is a 4-ounce pimento bottle.

CREAM SACHET I

¼ cup beeswax chips, lightly packed
¼ cup sweet almond oil
2 tablespoons distilled water
8 droppers cologne of your choice

Melt the wax in a double boiler over hot water. Using a wire whisk, add the oil slowly until wax and oil are blended. Continuing to whisk, pour in the water, then remove from heat and add the cologne. Whisk until thoroughly blended and pour while still warm into small containers. This is a nice way to carry a cologne with you on a trip. It won't spill.

CREAM SACHET II

To the above ingredients of beeswax, almond oil, and water, add 20 drops each of tincture of ambergris, musk, and civet; 1 drop oil of cloves, and 30 drops oil of orange. This is a delicious fragrance. The one tiny drop of cloves hides and then peeks out now and then when you least expect it. Don't leave it out.

CREAM SACHET III

This base has a deceiving texture. It looks mealy, but it goes on as sleekly as a raindrop. It's excellent for a massage cream, too, for it disappears into the skin at once.

¼ cup coconut oil
20 drops oil of lavender
20 drops tincture of musk
10 drops oil of rosemary
10 drops oil of orange
10 drops oil of bergamot

Measure the coconut oil into a container over hot water and just barely melt it. Then, blending with a wire whisk, add the essential oils.

The sachet will harden as it cools so it should be poured into a wide-mouthed opaque glass container. Keep tightly closed.

COLOGNE

To make the cologne in the following recipes, essential oils are added to alcohol and allowed to age. The alcohol used is vodka at 80 or 90 proof. As a rule of thumb, you can make a cologne by blending 1 part essential oil with 20 parts of alcohol. This of course is only a general rule, since the essential oils, being organic, are of different potencies.

After adding oil to alcohol, set the glass container in a dark place and be sure the container is tightly stoppered. It should be shaken often, once a day if you can remember it. And it should age anywhere from 3 months to a year. Some of the best perfumes are aged for 2 years.

Courage

I don't know if I could resist a man who wore this blend as an after-shave lotion. I'm sure I couldn't. It has power, yet suggests gentleness. It's shy, but implies strength. It would be a dandy present for someone who didn't know how nice they were.

To 1 cup of vodka add:

3 droppers oil of lavender

2 droppers oil of rosemary

1 dropper plus 10 drops oil of orange, lemon, and bergamot

3 droppers tincture of musk

5 drops oil of rose geranium

LEMON SMOKE
    To 1 cup of vodka, add:
    6 droppers oil of orange
    4 droppers oil of bergamot
    2 droppers oil of lavender
    2 droppers tincture of ambergris

VICTORIAN REBEL
    A long lasting, rich scent.
    To 1 cup of vodka, add 5 droppers each oil of rose geranium and oil of patchouli.

ZAAAAPO
    This scent makes you want to hug people who wear it—not to embrace them romantically, but just to hug them cheerfully.
    To 1 cup of vodka, add:
    5 droppers tincture of ambergris
    5 droppers tincture of musk
    5 droppers tincture of civet
    5 droppers plus 10 drops oil of orange
    5 drops oil of clove
    It's not easy making up names for scents. The names all get to the place where they sound phony. But as long as I worked at producing some good scents, I don't want to discard them just because I don't have names for them. So they're included here, without names. These were the top 8 out of my best 20, so you are getting a good bunch. These scent combinations can be used in any of the recipes in the book that call for scenting. You will only need to vary the amounts according to their usage. These

particular recipes are designed for use with 1 cup of vodka.

1. 8 droppers oil of bergamot
   5 droppers oil of lavender
   3 droppers tincture of musk

2. 3 droppers oil of bergamot
   2 droppers oil of lavender
   1 dropper oil of lemon verbena
   3 droppers tincture of ambergris
   3 droppers tincture of musk

3. 6 droppers oil of lavender
   3 droppers oil of clove
   1 dropper oil of bergamot
   1 dropper tincture of musk

4. 7 droppers oil of lavender
   6 droppers oil of clove
   2 droppers tincture of musk
   2 droppers tincture of ambergris

5. 10 droppers oil of cinnamon
   10 droppers oil of clove

6. 10 droppers essence of ylang-ylang
   5 droppers oil of patchouli
   5 droppers oil of rose geranium

7. 10 droppers oil of bergamot
   10 droppers oil of clove

8. 10 droppers oil of ambergris
   10 droppers oil of rhodium

SOAP MAKING

*M*AKING YOUR OWN SOAP isn't much more difficult than making a cake from raw materials. It does seem strange, though, to be using kitchen techniques and tools to make something with which to wash your body. In fact, it seems like magic to combine an evil-smelling, ugly-looking jar of lye with an equally unattractive batch of fat and come up with a beautiful bar of soap. Running quickly through the process, it goes like this: Fat (either tallow, lard, or oil) is heated in a pot until it reaches a certain temperature. In the meantime, lye is added to water in another container and its temperature is adjusted to suit the fat. Then the two are stirred together until they interact and become of a pudding-like consistency. This action is called "saponification." The "pudding" is then poured into molds, where it will harden and then age.

Homemade soap has several advantages over the commercial kind. The beneficial natural glycerine remains in the mixture rather than being removed. For very little money you can prepare the same type of soap that costs over a dollar a bar. And you can make it to fit your own personal whims as to color, scent, size, and enrichment.

One of my favorite methods for learning a completely new process is to jump right in and *do it*. Later on, I reason, I can go back and come up with the whys, wherefores, and what's happenings. So if you want to jump right in and *do it* with a combination of fat and lye, a simplified recipe for 2 bars of soap follows. It will give you a chance to go through the whole procedure and probably get you hooked on making your own soap. You will need a large enameled pot, a wooden spoon, and a thermometer.

Basic Procedure

Ingredients for your first bar of soap are:
- 1 cup distilled water
- 2 cups fresh lard
- 10 level teaspoons lye from a fresh can of lye

Note: Lye is available in supermarkets—usually in the household products section. Do not use a product labeled "drain cleaner." Lye does perform this function, but many drain cleaners have additives that would not be at all suitable for soap making. Pennwalt sells a brand called Lewis Lye. Indco Lye is another brand name. Lye is packaged in 13-ounce cans in both flakes and crystal form.

1. Prepare a mold. This recipe makes 2 bars of soap about the size of the plastic soap boxes used for camping trips. A kiddie-size shoe box will easily hold that amount, and it can then be cut into two bars. Line the box with a

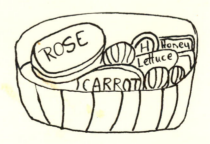

damp cloth, or with 2 layers of dampened brown paper cut from a grocery sack.

2. Prepare the lye solution. Pour the cup of water into a sturdy, quart-sized glass jar and stir in the 10 teaspoons lye. Lye fumes smell terrible, and the solution will burn if it gets on your skin, so do be very careful with it. Read the precautions on the can before working with it. If you spill a single flake on your body, wash it away with lots of water or water mixed with vinegar. Stir the lye until it is dissolved. The mixture will heat up immediately to about 200°F.; it will need to cool down to 85° F.

3. Measure the lard and put it into the enameled kettle. Place on a stove burner and slowly bring up the heat until the fat is melted. Remove from heat and cool to a temperature of 90° F.

4. When the lye mixture is at 85° F. and the fat is at 90° F., pour the lye very slowly and evenly into the pot of fat. I repeat, because it's important: *Add the lye to the fat.* The fat will turn pink when the lye is added. Then as you stir, it will begin to lighten, and eventually be a pure white color.

5. Stir with slow, even strokes until the mixture begins to thicken. You will, after a while, feel it begin to offer resistance to the spoon, and it will leave thin furrows behind in the wake of the spoon; if you lift a spoonful it will fall with a plop rather than a trickle. This means it is saponifying. It will take about 20 minutes, or maybe 30, for this to happen.

6. When the mixture feels like a thin pudding and looks satiny on its surface, pour it into the mold and immediately cover with towels to keep it warm. It mustn't cool too quickly.

7. Set aside for 24 hours. It should be firm, not necessarily hard, at this point. It can now be removed from the mold and cut into bars. It will then need to age at least 2 weeks before it is used.

If you've come this far, like what you see, and want to make soap in living color, enriched with brown sugar or cold cream, enlivened with glycerine, lettuce, or oatmeal, then you can read on. Or if your soap didn't turn out as you expected and you wonder what went wrong, reading on will help straighten things out so you can try again. Following is the extra information you will need to make full-sized batches.

More on Equipment

Most recipes in this section call for approximately 3 pounds of fat and will yield about 5 pounds of soap. This amount of fat will require a 7-quart kettle. Stainless steel, granite, or enameled pots may be used. Be sure there are no chips or cracks in the enamel. Lye will do terrible things to aluminum or tin.

The glass container used to mix the lye must be sturdy and free of flaws. The temperature rises so quickly when lye is added that a flawed jar could crack.

You will probably want to have two thermometers if you really get into soap making—one for the lye solution and the other for fats. You'll need the type that registers a wide range of temperatures. I like the ones used in photographic darkrooms. They are slender glass rods that register from a low of 10° F. to a high of 120° F. They cost about $1.50. Dairy thermometers work, too, if you

can find one. And metal meat thermometers, though I find them unwieldy.

A scale with good clear markings indicating ounces is a necessity. I purchased one described as a "diet scale." It registers up to 1 pound in both ounces and grams and costs less than $5.00.

A mold can be made of many things, but it must fulfill several requirements. It must hold the soap when it is in a liquid state, give shape to the mass, and keep the mixture from cooling too rapidly. The saponification process proceeds even after the soap is in the mold, and a sudden temperature drop can ruin the soap. Various-sized cardboard boxes are an excellent choice for molds. They can

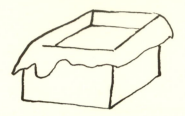

be lined with a wetted cloth or with heavy brown paper cut from grocery sacks. These can then be peeled away when the soap is ready. Be careful where you place your cardboard molds, because the lye can soak through the cardboard. Place it on several layers of newspaper to protect the surface underneath.

I have some interesting old embroidered dresser scarves that I sometimes lay in the bottom of my cardboard molds. When they are peeled away, an assortment of flowers, leaves, and birds decorate the surface of the soap. You can lay other patterned objects in the bottom of the mold, too, as long as they are made of substances that won't be affected by lye.

For small individual molds I use those ornate containers that hold cookies, cupcakes, and other fattening desserts. Plastic cottage cheese containers make nice fat bars, as do yogurt containers. They are flexible and can be peeled away from the soap. Molds can be rubbed with oil before filling.

When soap has firmed up so it can be lifted all in one piece, it is taken from the mold. It is then cut into bars with a serrated kitchen knife, or by using a piece of taut wire held between the two hands.

More on Processes

In soap making it is important to measure accurately and to observe temperature controls. The saponification process is one that depends on a chemical interaction, so the measurements and temperatures are quite important. It seems silly to make that statement since our forefathers made soap, a year's supply at a time, without ever looking at a thermometer or using a scale. Nevertheless, I don't seem to be able to do without them. In time, I suspect one would get past the need, but right now it's all a part of the necessary equipment. Measuring ingredients in ounces rather than in cups or spoons insures accuracy. One cup of an ingredient, for instance, does not necessarily weigh 8 ounces. The first recipe (page 124) is an exception. It is practically a foolproof formula so it's possible to be more casual with the measurements.

I should say a few words about stirring. Make the stirring slow and even—never brisk or hurried. It isn't necessary to keep the spoon in constant motion, though. I manage to read, sip coffee, and even get up and look out the window now and then during the stirring ritual.

Soap will generally show the first signs of thickening after 20 minutes. If your batch doesn't thicken within a reasonable time—say 45 minutes to an hour, you can examine the following ideas and act upon them. The soap may be too warm. You can set the kettle into a sink filled with cool water and continue to stir. Keep stirring, and if it doesn't thicken after 10 minutes you can try putting it back on the stove and heating it up to 110° F. Continue to stir as it heats, and don't bring the temperature up too quickly. Then turn the heat off and stir for another 20 minutes, or until it thickens. If it still doesn't thicken, pour it into the molds anyway. I have done this several times and awoke in the morning to find it had done its work overnight without me.

It takes some soaps longer than others to completely harden in the mold. If they begin to harden, you can assume they will continue to do so.

If soap curdles while you are making it, you're going to have to dump it. No amount of stirring, cajoling, or incanting over it will restore it. Curdling, in this instance, means that the mixture will take on a grainy look like soft rice floating in an unsavory-looking watery grease. There are several reasons why soap can curdle. Temperatures may have been off. The fat may have been rancid or contained salt, or the ingredients may not have been measured accurately.

When soap is properly made and properly aged, there will be no free alkali in it. This means the lye will have been changed into something else. When an alkali-free bar of soap is touched to the tongue, it will leave no burning sensation. Aging the soap is important. All soap needs at least two weeks to age after it comes out of the mold. If you see a dusty coating on its surface at this time, scrape it away before you wrap it. It won't hurt you, but it is drying to the skin.

Unperfumed soap doesn't have to be wrapped, but since I like to wrap mine I do. It's fun to make wrappings from all kinds of beautifully colored papers. Then I seal it with decorative seals that tell me later on what kind of soap is inside.

When recipes call for powdered soap or soap flakes, I

have used those described in the U.S.D.A. Bulletin No.
139. They are listed as being light-duty soap products as
opposed to heavy duty. This doesn't mean I'm endorsing
one brand over some other one. Any soap powder that is
unbuilt—that is, has no alkaline salts added to it—will serve
the purpose. It is also possible to buy powdered castile
soap from herbalists and possibly from a pharmacy.

Thoughts on Fats

Leftover kitchen drippings can be used for soap making,
as long as they are free of salt. Collect unsalty drippings
in a clean container in the refrigerator until you have
enough to make it worth while to work with. A 1-pound
coffee can, to give you an idea of volume, will hold 2
pounds of grease.

To prepare the drippings for use, put them into a
kettle and cover with clean water. This measurement
doesn't have to be precise, but I would suggest that the
fat be well covered by water. Heat the water and fat
together until the fat is all melted. Then put it in the refrigerator for several hours (or overnight) to allow the
clean fat to rise to the top while the debris sinks to the
bottom. When it is cool and the fat is in a semihard layer,
remove this top layer and scrape away any gelatinous
formation on its bottom. Now the fat can be sweetened
by putting it back into another pot of water. For every
quart of water you use to cover the fat, add 1 teaspoon
alum and 1 teaspoon baking soda. Bring this mixture to a
boil and let it boil for 5 minutes. Cool, then put it into the
refrigerator to harden. If the layer of cooled fat smells
fresh and sweet, it is now ready to use. If not, it can be

sweetened once again by the same process. Store it in a nice, clean jar until you're ready to use it.

You can buy scraps of fresh beef fat or mutton fat from the butcher and turn it into superior tallow for soap making. Tallow makes a pure, hard white soap. (Chicken fat is too soft, though small proportions of it can be used with other fats.) Some butcher shops will give you fat cuttings for nothing. Others will charge about 10 cents a pound. I buy a manageable amount—5 to 6 pounds at a time.

To prepare this fat for soap making, it will have to be processed in a bath to bring out the tallow. Cut the chunks of fat into pieces about the size of a walnut. Put them all into a big pot and cover the bottom of the pot with an inch or two of water to keep the fat from scorching at the beginning of the process. Set the pot over a slow fire and stir occasionally to keep it from sticking. It will take a long time to extract the tallow—5 to 6 hours. Look at it every now and then. You will see the pieces of fat gradually reduce in size as the tallow is drawn from them. At the end of the processing time, you will have a pot of liquid tallow with small pieces of scrap floating in it. Strain the liquid fat through a kitchen sieve covered with a cloth and put the clear liquid into the refrigerator to cool. When it is cool, the tallow will rise to the top in a rock-hard, white chunk. Scrape away any gelatinous layer from the bottom of the tallow and store for use.

Before you use any fats in soap recipes, be sure they are free of moisture. Either wipe away drops of water, or leave the fat out in the air long enough for the moisture to evaporate.

Some oils are used for soap making, too, as you will see from the following recipes. Along this line, you will observe that different fats call for different temperatures. Be sure to observe these temperatures for good results.

Scents and Color

Scents are added to the soap just before it is poured into the mold. Some recipes will give you exact amounts to use, but you can, of course, vary the amount to suit yourself. Use essential oils for scents; alcohol-based scents don't hold up. Just as a general rule of thumb, you can try 1 teaspoon of an essential oil (or 3 droppers) to a recipe that calls for 3 pounds of fat. This amount will be very mild.

Color is added just prior to pouring the soap into molds. See the section on color (pages 156–158) for information on natural coloring materials. The amount you use will depend strictly on your own preference.

The Recipes

The basic recipe (page 124), is easy to enlarge. Increase the ingredients to:

    48 ounces lard
    6½ ounces lye
    24 ounces distilled water
    Follow the basic procedure.

DEPENDABLE WHITE BAR

An all-tallow soap which can be used for the bath or for utility purposes. It is pure white, very hard, and long lasting. After it has aged, this soap can be powdered by rubbing it over a kitchen grater.

6½ ounces lye

24 ounces distilled water

48 ounces tallow

Using the basic procedure for soap making (pages 124–126), add the lye to the water and adjust the temperature to 98° F.

Melt the tallow and adjust the temperature to 110° F.

This makes 6 to 8 bars of soap. It can be given an appealing scent by adding 3 droppers oil of lavender plus 3 droppers oil of clove.

Olive-Almond Bars

A beautiful mild bar, enriched with almond meal. It's an excellent skin cleanser. Its color is golden.

6½ ounces lye

18 ounces distilled water

12 ounces olive oil

18 ounces lard or sweetened kitchen drippings

12 ounces coconut oil

2 ounces powdered almond meal

Scent: 4 droppers oil of bergamot

4 droppers oil of rhodium

Color: 10 drops yellow food coloring

Using the basic procedure for soap making (pages 124–126), add the lye to the water and adjust the temperature to 90 to 95° F.

The fats are heated together and cooled to 90 to 95° F.

Just before pouring the soap into molds, add the almond meal, scent, and color.

This recipe makes 10 to 12 large bars of soap. It has a pattern of birds, flowers, and leaves on its surface—the result of being poured into a mold with an embroidered cloth in it.

Bran or cornmeal, finely powdered, can be used in place of the almond meal.

LETTUCE SOAP

A clear, pale green soap that incorporates fresh lettuce in its formula. The lettuce acts as a deodorant and skin freshener. The lather is rich.

> 10 ounces lard
> 10 ounces distilled water
> 10 to 20 ounces lettuce
> 8 ounces coconut oil
> 3 ½ ounces lye
> 5 ounces distilled water
> Scent

The day before, prepare the lettuce-lard by simmering them together. Place the lard, 5 ounces distilled water, and the lettuce all together in an enameled pot. Put the lid on and simmer several hours until lettuce goes limp and the color becomes strong. Remove from the heat and pour through a strainer lined with cloth, then squeeze the cloth till all the juice is removed. Place in the refrigerator. After several hours, the lettuce-lard will rise to the top of the water in a firm layer. Remove this layer and scrape or pat away any excess moisture.

Check the weight before using in soap. If any weight has been lost, add plain lard to replace it.

Put the lettuce-lard (it will be pale green) back in the (clean) pot. Heat to melt, then adjust the temperature to 90° F.

Dissolve the lye in the 10 ounces distilled water and adjust the temperature to 85° F.

You can scent this if you like by adding:
  4 droppers oil of bergamot
  2 droppers oil of rose geranium

OPAQUE PATCHOULI

Patchouli bars are smooth to the touch and feel silky
on the skin. The fragrance is delicate but long lasting.
This low-lathering bar makes a beautiful gift. Wrap it in
some lavender tissue paper with golden seals on it.

  48 ounces tallow
  6½ ounces lye
  24 ounces distilled water
  8 ounces granulated sugar
  8 ounces 80-proof vodka
  4 droppers oil of patchouli

Using the basic procedure for soap making (pages
124–126), melt the tallow and adjust the temperature to
110° F.

Add the lye to 18 ounces of the distilled water and
adjust the temperature to 85° F.

In the meantime, dissolve the sugar in 6 oz. distilled
water and add the vodka. Heat to a temperature of 85° F.
—the same as the lye mixture.

When the soap begins to thicken and become glossy,
add the sugar-alcohol mixture. It will turn the mixture a
pure, satiny white. Then add the oil of patchouli and continue to stir until the mixture thickens. Pour into molds.

LEMON-GLYCERINE LIQUID

This is nice in the shower. When your body is wet
all over, squeeze out a few drops here and there and rub
it into a lather. Some people like this for a shampoo, too,

but I find the glycerine tends to make my hair feel gummy. It's very mild.

1 bar castile soap (enough to make 4 ounces)
1 pint distilled water
3 ounces glycerine
2 droppers oil of lemon
2 droppers oil of lime

Shave the castile soap and put, along with the distilled water, into the top of a double boiler over hot water. When melted, add the glycerine. Remove from the heat and stir in the oil of lemon and oil of lime.

I keep this mixture in a plastic bottle that once held liquid shampoo. It has a pour cap which makes it easy to use. It's a good way to carry soap on a trip, too.

SHAVING SOAP

A white, semifluffy mixture to fill somebody's shaving mug. This amount will fill 2 small mugs. It is frothy at first, so you will need to pour some and wait for it to settle down before you can add the rest of the batch.

½ cup Ivory soap powder
1 cup distilled water
2 tablespoons melted coconut oil
3 tablespoons sweet almond oil
1 tablespoon borax
Scent of your choice

Dissolve the soap by placing it in the cup of water and stirring. When dissolved, pour into a blender. Add the rest of the ingredients and blend until the mixture is fluffy. Add the scent. (For this recipe I like a mixture of 10 drops oil of patchouli and 10 drops oil of rose geranium.)

Peppermint Rice Soap

This recipe makes 6 small bars of glistening white, crispy-smelling soap with opaque rice shapes floating in it. It has a rich lather.

12 ounces Ivory bar soap
18 ounces powdered soap—either powdered castile or Ivory soap powder
9 ounces distilled water
12 ounces peppermint vodka
4 droppers oil of peppermint

Grate the bar soap and add to the powdered soap in the top of double boiler. (Note: Any soap slivers you have left over from cutting your own soap into bars can be used here in place of the Ivory bar. Be sure they have aged completely if you use them.) Add the distilled water and stir; the mixture will seem very dry. Bring the heat up slowly and stir the contents of the pot occasionally, keeping the lid on between stirrings. When the mixture becomes gummy and can be blended into a homogeneous mass, add the vodka and remove from the heat. Mix well, then add the peppermint oil. Pour into molds; it will be fairly stiff.

Peppermint vodka isn't really necessary. Plain will work just as well. I only used it because it seemed like a fun idea.

ALL-PURPOSE CLEANING GELÉE

A far-reaching, economical cleaning compound for dishes, laundry, or people. It makes up into about a gallon of quivering gelée. I put the bulk of it away on a cool shelf and keep a wide-mouthed quart of it handy for use.

3 quarts distilled or soft water
6 ounces Ivory soap bar, in shavings
2 ounces sal soda
2 tablespoons ammonia (cloudy or clear)

Put the water into an enameled kettle and add the soap shavings. Set over a low fire and simmer until the soap is dissolved. Add the sal soda and ammonia. Bring to a low boil and let boil for 10 minutes.

Remove from the fire, and when it has cooled a bit pour it into containers and store in a cool place. It will have the consistency of a gelatin pudding.

MARSHMALLOW OATMEAL BATH GELÉE

Use in place of soap. Wet the skin and rub the gelée in till it lathers. It feels creamy and luxurious.

¼ cup oatmeal flakes
1 cup Ivory soap powder
½ cup distilled water
3 droppers oil of bergamot
1 dropper oil of rhodium

Rub the oatmeal through a kitchen sieve to make it fine and powdery.

Put the soap powder and water in a stainless steel or glass bowl and let stand for 2 hours, or until they are blended and have a syrupy, fluffy consistency.

Stir in the oatmeal and the oil of bergamot and oil of rhodium.

To make a rich, frothy green, add 4 drops each of yellow and blue food coloring and stir.

Makes approximately 1 pint of gelée.

Low-Fat Face Scrubber

An excellent facial cleanser for anyone who doesn't want to use plain soap every day. It's somewhat like a facial, except that it's removed immediately. Its gentle, natural ingredients remove oil and grime.

> 4 ounces powdered oatmeal
> 2 ounces powdered almond meal
> 1 ounce powdered orrisroot
> 1 ounce powdered soap (Ivory soap powder or powdered castile)

Note: The soap you make can be reduced to a powder after it has aged. Simply grate it with the kitchen grater, using the smallest openings.

Mix all the ingredients. To apply, make a paste with about a tablespoon of it in the palm of your hand, plus warm water. Rub well into the skin till it lathers, then rinse with clear water. Repeat for a super-clean feeling.

Soap Bars from Kitchen Drippings

Be sure the fat you've collected is free from salt. Sweeten it according to the directions on page 131. This recipe makes about 5 pounds of good soap. The borax will aid its lathering properties.

> 6½ ounces lye
> 20 ounces distilled water

3 pounds kitchen drippings

⅛ cup borax

Following the basic procedures for soap making, add the lye to the water and adjust the temperature to 85° F.

Melt the drippings and adjust the temperature to 90° F. When the fats are at 90° F., add the borax and stir.

BROWN HONEY BARS

A beautiful, amber-colored bar enriched with honey. It smells musky and mysterious.

6½ ounces lye

20 ounces distilled water

40 ounces tallow

8 ounces coconut oil

2 ounces honey

Burnt-sugar coloring to suit your taste, but not over 2 ounces. (See the section on color, page 158.)

Scent of your choice

Using the basic procedures for soap making (pages 124–126), add the lye to the water and adjust the temperature to 110° F.

Melt the fats and adjust the temperature to 98° F.

Just before pouring into molds, add the honey, coloring matter and scent. (For this soap I like 3 droppers oil of bergamot plus 1 dropper oil of rhodium.)

CRISPY COCONUT

An ivory-white soap that will give nice, fat bubbles.

6½ ounces lye

20 ounces distilled water

20 ounces coconut oil

12 ounces lard

4 ounces olive oil

2 droppers oil of coconut

Using the basic procedures for soap making (pages 124–126), add the lye to the water and adjust the temperature to 75° F.

Melt the fats together and adjust the temperature to 85° F.

Add 2 droppers oil of coconut just before pouring the soap into molds.

Rosin Bars

This soap almost duplicates the fresh-smelling bars that people used to rub on a washboard. The rosin in the recipe adds a rich, brown color and increases the lathering properties of the soap. It is available from drugstores and from herbalists.

Use the Dependable White Bar recipe on page 133–134. You may use all tallow, or half tallow and half lard.

Add 4 ounces of powdered rosin to the fat at the time you put it on the stove to melt. Rosin melts slowly. Mash and press any lumps until all are dissolved.

Rosy-Glycerine Soap

This will not have a rich lather, but will be a firm, glossy bar that is extremely gentle. The extra glycerine is added for its emollient qualities.

    48 ounces tallow
    6½ ounces lye
    24 ounces distilled water
    2 ounces glycerine
    Coloring of your choice
    2 droppers oil of rose geranium
    1 dropper oil of verbena

Prepare soap by using the basic procedures (pages 124–126); the tallow is heated to melt and then adjusted to a temperature of 110° F. The lye is dissolved in water and the temperature adjusted to 98° F.

After the soap begins to thicken slightly in the pot and becomes glossy, slowly pour in the glycerine. Continue to stir and blend.

To add rosy color, add food coloring to suit or use alkanet root. (See the section on color, pages 156–158.) Then add the scent.

Brown Sugar Transparent Soap

Beautiful bars of the palest brown. They are scented with rose and a woodsmoke fragrance.

    6½ ounces lye
    17 ounces distilled water
    6 ounces brown sugar
    12 ounces 80-proof vodka
    14 ounces glycerine
    20 ounces lard
    10 ounces coconut oil
    2 droppers oil of rhodium
    1 dropper oil of rose geranium

Following the basic procedure for making soap (pages 124–126), dissolve the lye in the water.

In another container, dissolve the brown sugar in the vodka. Stir until completely dissolved, then add the glycerine. Add this mixture to the lye solution and adjust the temperature to 90° F.

Melt the lard and coconut oil together and adjust the temperature to 90° F.

When both solutions are at 90° F., add the lye mixture to the fat mixture, stirring slowly and continuously. When it begins to thicken, add the scent and pour into molds.

Cover the molds quickly and allow 24 hours before you peek at them. Remove from the molds when the soap has set—this may take more than the usual 24 hours. It will need to age to take on its full transparent appearance.

GATHERING AND EXTRACTING THE FRAGRANCE OF PLANTS

*I*F YOU GROW HERBS and flowers or gather them from the countryside, you can preserve their essence in either a dried form or in the form of an oil. These materials can then be used in such things as potpourris, sachets, cosmetics, and cologne.

Gathering Plant Material

As a general rule, all plants should be gathered when they're at their peak. This means they are collected when they first begin to flower, for at this point they contain the most readily available essential oils. Cut the plants early in the morning, in that period after the sun has dried the morning dew but before it has a chance to dehydrate the plants.

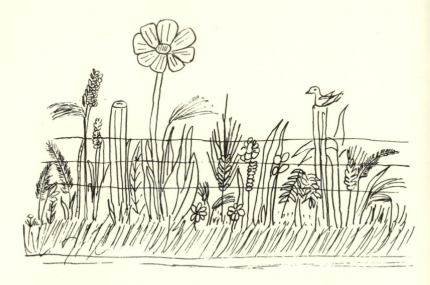

LEAVES

When only the fragrant leaves of a plant are desired, the stalks should be cut when the leaves are young and newly formed. Tired, yellow, wilted leaves should be left outside to die a natural death.

ROOTS

The roots of plants that are fragrant, like peony, angelica, sweet flag, lovage, or Spanish iris (orris), should be gathered in the fall for superior results. They can, however, be taken up in the early spring with fair results. The roots are dug and then scrubbed thoroughly to remove garden soil.

FLOWERS

Flowers are collected when they reach full maturity. Examples of those gathered for their fragrance and color are lavender, rose buds, chamomile, calendula, and safflower.

Drying and Storing

The main thing to remember about drying plant material is that it should be kept clean and dry. It should be dried as quickly as possible by natural means. This means you keep one step ahead of mold. You can't heat it up quickly or you will be treating it like skin is treated when its gets a quick, damaging sunburn.

Materials should be cleaned before they go into a drying process and then should be kept clean. You wouldn't want to take a bath with dirty chamomile or rosemary.

LEAVES

Leaves can be dried by picking the leaves from the stem before drying, or the leaves can be dried with the stems on and then picked off after they are dry. If you prefer to dry just the leaves, throw away any unhealthy-looking leaves and wash the goodies in gently running water.

Because you will want the leaves to dry quickly in order to retain their fragrance, you will want them to receive air and warmth, but not bright sunlight. Devise a screen or use a spare window screen, which can be sus-

pended off the ground. This will allow the air to move around, under, and through it. A layer of cheesecloth under and over the leaves discourages insects and unruly breezes. Spread leaves on the screen so they're not more than an inch thick. If you dry them outside, bring them in each evening so they won't be subjected to the night's dampness. If you have an attic or some other dry spare corner, leaves can be dried inside on the same screens. Stir them each day to speed the process.

Leaves are dry when they feel crispy and can be crumpled between the fingers. It's not possible to say exactly how long this takes, for it depends on the weather, the leaf, and other drying conditions. It may be as little as 4 days or it may take 2 to 3 weeks.

When leaves are left on the stem to dry, the stems are rinsed, thoroughly shaken, and then tied into small bunches so they can be suspended. They are tied at the root end so they will hang head down. An attic is a perfect spot for this type of drying, for bright sunlight can't reach the plants, yet there is a natural supply of dry, circulating heat. If the attic is dusty, place each bunch inside a perforated grocery sack; they will be protected from dust, yet the air can still circulate around them. Pull the sack down loosely over the bunches, which will hang head down inside the bag. Check every day or so at the beginning of the process to guard against mold. You can fluff the stems and separate them from each other.

When leaves are crispy dry, they are picked from the stems and stored.

To store, choose light-tight containers with nicely fitted lids. Be sure to label the containers. All dried leaves can look alike after a while, and your nose may not be able to sort out one fragrance from another.

ROOTS

Since roots are thick and fleshy, they will need to be divided before they are dried. Wash the root to remove all dirt and debris; you may have to use a brush. Cut the root into slices ¼ to ½ inch thick. Place the cut roots on drying screens such as those for leaves. Or roots can be started outside to remove the initial moisture and then the process can be continued in the oven. Lay the slices on cookie sheets and keep the oven temperature down to 175° F. Even then it's good to keep the oven door slightly ajar. You can test for dryness by snapping the sliced root in half. When it is dry, it will break with a brittle, cracking sound.

Roots should be stored in the same fashion as leaves—in

light-tight (preferably glass) containers with close-fitting lids.

FLOWERS

Flowers are gathered both for their fragrance and their color. They are dried by the same method as that for leaves, except they need to be handled more gently. To preserve their color, be especially careful not to expose them to direct sunlight. It will drain them of color very quickly.

Store flowers as leaves are stored. After a week's time check the container to see if any droplets of moisture have formed. If so, take the flowers out and give them several more days in the open air before they're put back into storage containers.

Though you will want to store the flower material in the dark until you're ready to use it, I like to fill up one glass jar with layers of blossoms and petals, and keep it out in the open where I can see it. I use violet leaves, violets, chamomile blossoms, rose petals, or whatever other beautiful blossoms come my way. They lose their color eventually but they make me happy while they're doing it.

Extracting and Preserving Fragrances

I don't know why extracting fragrance from a plant is such an exciting process. I suppose part of the fun lies in the fact that such a humble process can produce such elegant results. The fragrance can be extracted in several ways, one of them involving the use of a still. But in this section I'll describe the most simple ones—ones that require the use of vegetable oils or household fats. The oils resulting from these procedures can be used to scent your body, to add to incense, bath water—wherever, in fact, a recipe calls for an essential oil. They will be milder than commercially produced essential oils, but they will be uniquely yours.

EXTRACTING FRAGRANCE WITH FAT

Process I
> 1 cup pure, fresh lard
> 2 teaspoons tincture of benzoin
> 1 clean 1-pound coffee tin or similar container with a lid
> Clean cheesecloth
> Fragrant material of your choice
> 2 drops oil of sandalwood

To make the absorbent base, warm the lard just enough to melt it and add the tincture of benzoin.

Pour the lard into the coffee tin and allow to cool. You will have a layer of fat about 2 inches deep.

In the meantime, gather the flowers you plan to use for fragrance. (You can choose from the list of fragrant materials on pages 78–79.) You will need enough material to fill the space in the container not taken up by the fat.

After the lard has solidified, make a loosely fitting liner from the cheesecloth. This makes a "bag" into which you'll place the flowers. The bag can be pulled out and emptied as you replace old flowers with new.

Fill the bag with petals and put the lid back on the container. Every other day for 3 weeks, replace old flowers with new ones. Don't worry if you miss a day or if you go one week over or one week less. It only means the scent will be a bit stronger or weaker. You can use whatever flowers are in season, using just one or mixing and matching as you choose.

At the end of the absorption time, remove the lard from the container by heating it gently over water. Strain it through several layers of cheesecloth and add the oil of sandalwood. Pour into pretty storage containers and label them.

This mixture can now be used as a scented cream to soften the skin, as a massage cream, or as a cream sachet.

Or it can be further processed to make a scented liquid. You can call this "cologne" or you can call it a "water." It will smell wonderful no matter how it's labeled.

After the lard has been processed, and has solidified, chop it into bite-sized pieces and drop them into a wide-mouthed quart jar. (Do not add fixative at this point to lard you plan to treat in this fashion.) Pour 1 cup of pure alcohol over it and cap tightly. (I use Everclear, a product that is 90 percent pure alcohol. It's sold in liquor stores.)

Keep the jar handy so it can be shaken every day for 2 weeks to a month. Or the jar can simply be stored away in a dark corner for 3 months. This aging period is necessary to transfer the scent from the lard to the alcohol. You can test its fragrance at the end of two weeks to see if you want to stop or continue. When the scent is satisfactory, add 4 drops oil of sandalwood as a fixative and pour into pretty cologne bottles that can be tightly stoppered.

PROCESS II

Fat can be cut from uncooked roasts, chops, and so forth and processed to make fresh, clean tallow to replace the lard in the above recipe. The procedure for creating clean tallow from fat is found in the section on soap, page 132.

Replace the cup of lard in recipe I with 1 cup of this pure tallow.

Instead of using a coffee can as a container for impregnating the lard or tallow with fragrance, you can select two containers which are exactly the same size—pie tins, for instance, or shallow mixing bowls. Melt the fat and pour one-half into each container. After it hardens, fill both containers with scented material and invert one over the other so they form a good seal. If you wish, you can tape the edges, but I usually just lay a weight over the top to keep the two in contact. Change the material every other day and follow the same procedure as for extraction recipe I.

EXTRACTING FRAGRANCE WITH OIL

To extract fragrance from plant material with oil, a fixed oil such as safflower, sweet almond, or olive oil is used. Olive oil is a favorite of many people, but I find its basic odor too strong.

What you're doing in this process is coaxing the essential oils out of the plant material and incorporating them into your choice of a fixed oil (above).

PROCESS I

Drop clean fresh cotton balls into a wide-mouthed quart glass jar to form a layer 2 inches deep. Saturate the cotton with oil by pouring one of the above oils over it and stirring until it is saturated. When the balls are saturated, fill the jar to the top with flowers.

I like to use lilacs because they are so springlike. I pull the blossoms from the stems and pack them in tightly. It takes a huge armful of blossoms to fill the jar. Screw the lid on tightly and set the jar in the sun to keep it warm. Since lilacs bloom early in the spring, there are many cool, wet days, so I take advantage of the floor registers in our old house, keeping the bottle on the register on rainy days. The blossoms are replaced every third or fourth day or whenever the blooms look tired. I continue to replace and refill for as long as lilacs last—usually three weeks of full bloom. If lilies of the valley come into bloom at this time, I sometimes combine the two flowers in the jar.

When you're satisfied with the fragrance, remove the cotton balls and squeeze out every last drop of the oil into a small opaque glass vial with a good cork. Or use a dark glass bottle with a screw-top lid. This recipe will give you 3 or 4 ounces of oil. Add 1 drop of an animal fixative (ambergris, civet, or musk) for each ounce of oil. Or add 1 teaspoon liquid storax. It has a special affinity for flower fragrances.

PROCESS II

In the top of a double boiler, place 1 cup of oil of sweet almond or safflower oil. Allow the oil to warm, but don't permit it to actually become hot. (You should be able to stick your finger in it.) Now add as much flower material as the pot will hold, and put the lid on the pot. Let it sit for 2 hours over heat, but don't "cook" the plants; they only need to be kept warm. Now, remove the plant material with a slotted kitchen spoon. Squeeze the oil out of the plants back into the pot. (It won't hurt if you leave some material in the oil.) Add a new batch of flowers every 2 hours, all day long. In fact, I sometimes repeat this process for 2 days if the fragrance doesn't seem strong enough. When satisfied with the scent, leave the last batch of material in the pot and place it over direct heat. Allow it to come to a boil, then reduce the heat to a simmer. This will remove the moisture from the oil. When the plant material is crispy, strain through a cloth. Add 1 teaspoon tincture of benzoin and 1 teaspoon liquid storax. Store in dark, well-stoppered bottles.

COLOR, AND
HOW TO GET IT

*T*HERE ARE SEVERAL WAYS to add color to soaps, creams, bath products, and so on. The food colorings used for such things as icings are nice because they can be added a drop at a time and you can watch them as they develop. The only problem is that if you add too much the color will not only be in the product, but indelibly stenciled on your body. I wore one bright green arm and one regular skin-colored one for three long days one summer. Eventually it wore off, but I walked around feeling like a half-dead house plant. It is also possible to order dyes from color-supply houses. But when I investigated this possibility, I discovered I would have to order such massive amounts that it wouldn't be practical. Fortunately, there are a number of natural materials that can be used to give color. None of them, by the way, will give you a bright green arm.

Grass, spinach, beet tops or other edible greens can all be used. Caution: Don't use any greens that you wouldn't want to eat. Rhubarb leaves, for instance, are poison if eaten. I don't know that they would necessarily be poisonous in a hand cream, but it's not worth the risk to find out. Choose the green material you want, bruise it, and pack enough of it in a pint jar to completely fill it. Pour in a cup of 80-proof vodka and cap the bottle. Mash and stir it every day for a week. Then, at the end of the week, strain away the clear liquid color through several layers of cloth. The color, of course, will be green.

The same green materials can have their color extracted by simmering them in distilled water. Bruise the greenery, place it in an enamel pan, and just barely cover it with water. Simmer and stir until color develops. In order to get full, concentrated color, simmer until the liquid is half used up. Strain through cloth and then bottle for use. Keep refrigerated if you're not going to use it right away.

When recipes call for any kind of fats that require heating—lard, coconut oil, and so on—the green materials (above) can be heated right with the fat and then strained away later. To each ounce of fat, add at least an equal amount of green material. For deeper shades of green I add double the amount of plant material. See the recipe for Lettuce Soap (page 135) for more complete information.

Many herbs and spices give colors, too. Alkanet root, (which can be purchased from herbalists) makes beautiful, clear shades of brown when steeped in water. Simmer ½ ounce of the herb in 1 cup distilled water for 5 minutes, then strain and keep in the refrigerator until ready for use. Just 2 teaspoons of this "tea" will color 1 cup of bath oil. Steeped in alcohol rather than water, alkanet root will give shades from pink to scarlet. Put ½ ounce in a ½-pint bottle and fill it with 80-proof vodka. Shake several times a day for a week. Strain when ready to use.

Saffron is a very expensive herb, so you probably won't be using it often. But just a pinch of it will deliver a strikingly bright yellow or orange. Extract the color by placing a pinch of saffron in a glass jar; a small spice container will do. Pour boiling water over it and shake every day for several days to develop full color, although it can be used the same day. Strain before using. Two droppers of this solution will color approximately 6 ounces of liquid.

Safflower can be used in the same way as saffron (above). Safflower is, in fact, often used as a substitute for the more expensive saffron.

The spice tumeric will give a rich yellow. Extract the color by steeping it in either water or alcohol. Place a teaspoon in a glass jar and follow the directions for saffron (above).

Burnt sugar will give varying shades of caramel and brown. Place ½ pound granulated sugar in a skillet and leave it until it turns black and crispy. Turn off the heat and pour a cup of water over it. Let it steep for five minutes, stirring the mixture as it steeps, then strain through a cloth and keep cool until ready to use.

SOURCE LIST

WILDFLOWER SEEDS AND PLANTS

Gardens of the Blue Ridge
  Ashford, McDowell County
  North Carolina 28603
  (Free price list.)

Leslie's Wildflower Nursery
  30 Sumner Street
  Methuen, Massachusetts 01844
  (25 cents for price list.)

Three Laurels
  Madison County
  Marshall, North Carolina 28753
  (Free price list.)

Woodland Acres Nursery
  Crivetz, Wisconsin 54114
  (10 cents for price list.)

BOTANICALS, ESSENTIAL OILS, AND GUMS

Indiana Botanic Gardens
    P.O. Box 5
    Hammond, Indiana 46325

Nature's Herb Company
    281 Ellis Street
    San Francisco, California 94102

Herb Products Company
    11012 Magnolia Boulevard
    North Hollywood, California 91601

Wide World of Herbs, Ltd.
    11 St. Catherine Street East
    Montreal, 129, P.Q., Canada

BIBLIOGRAPHY

Bergen, J. Y. *Elements of Botany*. Boston: Ginn & Co., 1897.

Birdseye, Clarence and Eleanor G. *Growing Woodland Plants*. New York: Oxford Univ. Press, 1951.

Brown, Alice Cook. *Early American Herb Recipes*. New York: Bonanza Books, 1966.

Clarkson, Rosetta E. *Herbs: Their Culture and Uses*. New York: Macmillan, 1945.

Culpeper, Nicholas. *Culpeper's Complete Herbal*. London: W. Foulsham & Co. Ltd. Reprint of a seventeenth-century publication.

De Bairacli Levy, Juliette. *Herbal Handbook for Everyone*. Newton, Mass.: Charles T. Branford Co., 1967.

Fox, Helen Morgenthau. *Gardening with Herbs for Flavor and Fragrance*. New York: Dover Publications, 1970. Reprint of the 1933 Macmillan edition.

McCleod, Dawn. *Herb Handbook*. North Hollywood, Calif.: Wilshire Book Co., 1968 and 1972.

Meyer, Joseph E. *The Herbalist*. Privately printed in 1918. Distributed by Indiana Botanical Gardens, Hammond,

Indiana. Revised and enlarged in 1960 by Clarence Meyer. Copyright Clarence Meyer 1973.

Rhode, Eleanor Sinclair. *A Garden of Herbs*. New York: Dover Publications, 1969.

GLOSSARY

The following are some terms which may be unfamiliar to you. They are explained in relation to the way they are used in this book.

ESSENTIAL AND FIXED OILS: An essential oil is one which has been expressed from plants. It contains the plant's properties and odor. Examples would be oil of lemon, oil of nutmeg, oil of lavender. Essential oils can be purchased from herbal and botanical outlets. They are volatile, i.e., they evaporate rapidly. Fixed oils, on the other hand, are manufactured oils such as sesame, olive, coconut, etc., which are fixed so they are not volatile. They can be purchased at the supermarket.

FIXATIVE: A substance added to fragrant materials to blend and hold the fragrance together. Examples are orrisroot or gum benzoin.

GUM ARABIC (ACACIA GUM): A powder which can be dissolved in water to make a good adhesive. In this book it is used in incense recipes. It is available from both druggists and herbalists.

LANOLIN: An oily, strong smelling substance derived from the wool of sheep. It has superior emollient qualities. It is available from druggists.

SAL TARTAR (POTASSIUM CARBONATE): An old fashioned term for potash or potassium carbonate. It was obtained from wood ashes and then used in making soap. Now it is chemically produced. It is available from druggists.

SALTPETER (NITRATE OF POTASSIUM): A chemical substance used as a preservative in meats, in medicine, and (in this book) as an ingredient in incense materials. It helps to ignite them and to regulate their burning. It is available from both druggists and herbalists.

STORAX (STYRAX): A resin extracted from trees of the genus Styrax. Traditionally it was used as an incense ingredient. It can be purchased from herbalists.

TARTARIC ACID: A plant derivative which is used in effervescent drinks and certain drug products. Available from druggists.

TINCTURE: A solution made by adding substances such as herbs, flowers, or animal products to alcohol and thereby extracting some of their properties. An example would be tincture of ambergris or tincture of benzoin. Tinctures are available from drugstores or herbalists.

INDEX

Beverly Plummer

Beverly Plummer, lecturer and authority on folk music, arts, and crafts, is a longstanding practitioner of the American pioneer's philosophy of "make-it-or-do-without." Her creations and lectures help spread this philosophy, as do her articles in magazines and Sunday supplements. Beverly and John Plummer create all their own household cleaners and cosmetics; they also grow in their backyard garden more than enough vegetables to feed themselves and a host of friends. Mrs. Plummer's previous books were *Give Every Day a Chance*, published in 1970, and *Earth Presents*, in 1973.